Mita Castle-Kanerova was born in Karlovy Vary, Czechoslovakia. In 1968, the year Russia sent troops into Czechoslovakia, she was in England on holiday and then became a political exile, unable to return to her country for twenty years. She teaches Social and Political Science at the Polytechnic of North London. She lives in London with her fourteen-year-old-daughter, now making frequent trips home to Prague. *High Hopes* is her first book.

HIGH HOPES

Young Voices from Eastern Europe

Mita Castle-Kanerova

Published by VIRAGO PRESS Limited 1992
20-23 Mandela Street, Camden Town, London NW1 0HQ

Copyright © 1992 Mita Castle-Kanerova

The right of Mita Castle-Kanerova to be identified as author of this Work has been asserted by her in accordance with the Copyright, Designs and Patents Act 1988

A CIP catalogue record for this book is available from the British Library

Printed in Great Britain by Cox & Wyman Ltd., Reading, Berkshire

To Zoya, my fourteen-year-old daughter

CONTENTS

Preface	ix
Acknowledgements	x
Introduction	xi

ROMANIA   1

Magdalena Sava, MY BRAVE FATHER	5
Ciobanu Oana, OUR HEROES	7
Nica Dan, MEMORIES OF THE REVOLUTION	9
Bugeanu Anca, BLOODSTAINED DECEMBER	11
Petrică Răzvan, IMPRESSIONS OF THE REVOLUTION	14
Macaşoi Marius, THE REVOLUTION ON 22 DECEMBER 1989	15
Codîrleanu Cristina, IN LOVE WITH FREEDOM	17
Gârgău Maria, COMPOSITION WITHOUT A TITLE, OR DISCOVERY	18
Dina Adriana, AN END COVERED IN BLOOD	20
Alina Roşca-Stănescu, THINGS THAT SHOULDN'T BE FORGOTTEN	23

GERMANY   25

From the magazine *Menschenskinder*	29
Angela Kunze, MY DIARY	34
Anke Höhne, IT'S OVER!	53
Katrin Klatt, THE OLD MEN	56
Peggy Einenkel, THE YEAR OF CHANGES	57

CZECHOSLOVAKIA 67
Marek Šváb, WE WANT ANSWERS! 71
Anonymous, LIES AND MORE LIES 72
Lenka Bárczayová, GREAT BEGINNING AND THE HARD TIMES TO COME 74
Tomáš Brzobohatý, 'THIS' IS WHAT WE CALL A REVOLUTION 77
Jana Kovačová, BEFORE, THEN AND NOW 104
Petr Tůma, FREEDOM AT A PRICE 112

POLAND 117
Ingelin Blix, THE NIGHTMARE OF THE MARTIAL LAW 121
Beata Pyka, MERCIFUL LORD, WE NEED YOUR HELP! 124
Magdalena Pawelczyk, A CHANGE – BUT WHAT NEXT? 130

HUNGARY 133
Anonymous, IS THIS DEMOCRACY? 137
Anna Radnóti, NO CHANGE 141
Péter Vági, Olívia Thuma, János Ungár, Eszter Vági and Mazsi Barna, DOES ONE NEED TO BELONG? 145
Péter Kolosi, Fruzsina Sánoor and Klara Dobrev, OUR OVER-POLITICISED PAST 155

THE SOVIET UNION 159
Katya Kalinina, THE RUSSIAN WHITE HOUSE UNDER BARRICADES 163
Ludmila and Maria Ozerov, THE DAYS THAT SHOOK THE WORLD 167
Anna, WAKING UP TO AN UNKNOWN FUTURE 169

PREFACE

This is a very personal journey through Eastern Europe. The collection of stories by young people is random, originating from talks and chats with friends, acquaintances and often relatives. There was no systematic search guiding it. To those who would have liked to contribute but could not, I express my apologies. But there is hope that this first attempt at capturing and documenting the young people's lives in the part of the world that is changing so rapidly will spark a wave of curiosity that will open up greater communication. After reading some of the more sober or the more passionate accounts offered here, one wants to know more. The hardship, the happiness, the confusions of the young people of Eastern Europe can't, I feel, but be also our own.

ACKNOWLEDGEMENTS

This book involved the help of many friends and acquaintances. I would like to express my warmest thanks to Lennie Goodings who involved me in the project in the first place. She conceived of the idea and continued to give me her support. Many thanks go to Reini and Elke Wandel for their help with the East German stories and to Miranda Kirby, Monica Rorison and Nick Shepherd, the translators from German; to Julia Szalai in Budapest who organised my conversations with the Hungarian contributors; to Halina Cieplinska in Warsaw, who alerted some of her friends, and Alicja Iwana Kronenberg who translated from Polish; to Anna Fielder, who contacted her friends in Bucharest, and to the translator Tatiana Roșca-Stănescu who translated the Romanian stories; to my mother Zdeňka Kaněrová, who enthused some of my old teachers, which resulted in a couple of the Czech stories I was happy to translate; to Pieta Monk who brought the Russian stories from Moscow; and to all those contributors whose accounts we were unable to publish: Petra Horecká, Stanislava Novotná, Radim Mrázek, Helena Ondrůšková, Lenka Šafarová, Jirka Lukeš, Magda Štorkova, Will Firth, Yvonne Zitzmann, Piotr Bucki, Patricia Radoi and many of the young Romanian people who wrote from the same school as those published here.

Thanks go also to those who helped to produce the book.

INTRODUCTION

I could not believe my eyes when the stories started arriving in the post. This is not a collection of short stories written by young people of what was commonly called Eastern Europe – it is a political and historical testimony. Consciously or unconsciously, these people have recorded a piece of history. Sometimes even the most skilful historians can't reach that depth of emotion and feeling. These writers reveal a sense of personal responsibility to tell the world what it was like to live under a regime called 'communism': a dying monster to some, a benign but friendless animal to others.

Here is an insight into the everyday fears, hopes, disappointments and confusions about what that regime actually did to them, the thirteen- to twenty-seven-year-olds, what it did to their parents or grandparents, and where they are all going now with the proclaimed death of a political system that ruled over them for the past forty-odd years, and seventy or so years in the Soviet Union itself, where it all began. They pose questions that could shame many politicians: about collective guilt, about corruptibility, about the meaning of democracy, about the present-day 'goodies' as opposed to yesterday's 'baddies' not giving a toss about the people once more. Is the system really dead? Does it not live on in our consciousness, our habits, our way of life?

I was invited to a café in north London by Lennie Goodings of Virago. She told me about her plans to put together a collection by 'young voices of Eastern Europe'. A Canadian being interested in Eastern Europe? Well, everything is possible but I was a bit sceptical. How do you reach these young people (avoiding the most privileged, those who know the media game by now) who have been in the forefront of their sometimes dramatic, sometimes less dramatic revolutions that swept Eastern Europe since 1989? I was conscious that there are those whose stories have already been forgotten. The world wants to hear sensational news, and even though this collection was intended for young readers in the English-speaking world, how do you present the 'ordinariness' of life in a totally different society from the western one? We talked, and I agreed to help. I could not have done otherwise. I came to England twenty-three years ago. My home country is Czechoslovakia.

Being an exile has its own advantages and disadvantages. You are a perpetual outsider, which can sharpen your view of things. I am only too aware of the incomplete and often exaggerated picture of Eastern Europe that the western reader has. But I am also an outsider back home now: living in the 'no man's land'. So when the opportunity came and I could travel back to Czechoslovakia, I was nervous. It represented twenty years of not hearing the language around me, of not knowing whether I would fit in any more, whether I had any friends left. Funnily, my fears were not dissimilar to what appears in some of the stories: uncertainty about belonging because the system has just collapsed; a perpetual search. These young people, too, it seems, had known a kind of no man's land.

It undoubtedly started when Gorbachev came to power in the Soviet Union in 1985. I watched the news and secretly thought: 'this will mean me going back home'. When, and how, was completely unthinkable. The regime had its good days and its bad days; it had liberal periods, but it could also deliver its brutal clampdown blows, like in 1968 when Czechoslovakia was invaded and I became stranded on holiday in Britain. One must not trust the smiling faces, one must not trust the easing up of its grip – this could be a trap. That is where my thoughts and the thoughts of the generation that followed after me, these young people who write their stories here, merge. We grew up in a world where politics meant nasty surprises, where neighbours watched behind their lace curtains, where our parents shut themselves off either because of the pain that was inflicted on them or through 'not wanting to do us further damage'. Politics was thrust upon us, whether we liked it or not. But then, there were new hopes and new scepticism. One of my favourite Czech writers of the sixties, Ludvik Vaculik, summed up the source of this scepticism and the bullying that the small countries of Eastern Europe had to endure for so long: 'should Moscow now order us to be allowed freedom, I'll resist.'

Well, my concealed hope came true in 1988, when for the first time, the Czech secret police somehow, somewhere decided that it might not be such a bad thing to let me go home. Could one say that they began to be unsure of themselves? With hindsight, maybe . . . I took my daughter Zoya, then eleven years old. It was to be her very first meeting with her Czech family and relatives. We spend a frantic Christmas holiday there, trying to divide our time between all the branches of our rather extended family clan. We came back exhausted. A few days later I asked Zoya what she thought of her visit. She replied with a seriousness that I have not seen in her up to now: 'Well, mother,' she said, 'I know that the country is poor, but the people there are rich.' I loved her for those few words very, very dearly. We came closer to each other. Within the next two years we were travelling to Czechoslovakia together again, this time for three and a half months at a time when Czechoslovakia was well into its 'velvet revolution'. That was where my collection of stories began.

This perhaps explains the slight bias towards Czechoslovakia in the book. I must say so because I do not wish to be accused of Czech nationalism. Not now, no!

I was in Prague, teaching. It all happened like a fairytale. I was back, I was not a tourist, I had to make ends meet from a Czech salary, I was living with my daughter in the students' halls of residence, we travelled to work and school on the overcrowded public transport. I set about hustling friends and often relatives to write about their experiences in 1989. At the beginning it didn't go very well. I had promises, but no delivery. I felt awkward because I thought that of all the countries of Eastern Europe, this was the one from which I ought to be able to get at least a few stories. Then one day a window-cleaner came to the halls, and started cleaning the single window in my room with the precision and deliberation of a scientist. We began talking. He was a second-year medical student, earning extra cash. Cleaning my window took him a full four hours, during which time we discussed everything, from past to present. I asked him to write it down. I literally stood over him to finish the last few sentences before my final departure. He was Petr Tůma. Next, after we arrived back in England, came a letter from another student who participated in the events of 17 November, the night of the clashes with the police in Prague and the start of the 'revolution'. He had responded to a poster I pinned on various noticeboards. He wrote the longest piece, and I fell in love with his sensitivity, the deep appreciation of humanity that only the East Europeans possess, after having to ask themselves the fundamental question: 'who am I?' I was unable to shorten his story, so the full version takes up a good chunk of the book.

Then a second cousin of my daughter, Jana, spent a month with us and, hearing me talk of the book, she remarked: 'yes, we had to grow up very quickly, our generation is now in it all on its own.' Out of that conversation grew her piece.

But there are other stories, so wonderful in their variety,

their contrasting vision of the events that these people experienced together as friends, like the Hungarians.

There, I had no success at all to begin with. So it was arranged that I go to Budapest and talk to some of the young people there. I could not have done that without the superb organisational help of a friend, Julia, and her two children. I arrived on a Friday evening, after work, and two brothers, who wish to be anonymous, were waiting for me in a café on Saturday morning. I didn't need to ask any questions. They just talked. True enough, they selected themselves on the basis of being able to speak English, but otherwise they were as ordinary kids as one might expect in a thriving East European capital. What was striking, though, was their political sharpness. These 'kids' just didn't put up with any bullshit. They didn't speak about the niceties of the past or the present. They didn't have many illusions left, but neither were they overly pessimistic. This is the new generation of realists. The same experience repeated itself with the second, third and fourth groups I saw before departing at Sunday lunchtime, having seen just three or four Budapest cafés and Julia's flat, with sandwiches and hospitality that draws you back.

Stories from East Germany, or what was East Germany, were received, interestingly, with the highest degree of organisational precision. I contacted two of my long-standing West German friends living in Berlin, Reini and Elke. They placed an advert in one of the more radical journals reaching to different parts of now united Germany, and within a short time received a collection of stories, accounts and diaries. The need to talk speaks for itself, nourished by the double confusions, mixed feelings, personal crisis points when confronted with the question: 'what is a homeland?'

Poland is the country that kept escaping us. Though both Lennie and myself contacted numerous people and friends, the stories that came back were fewer than we expected.

What is here is a tale of hardship and impoverishment, reinforcing what I have heard on a number of occasions throughout Eastern Europe: 'it is the decent folk who always end up the worst.' But there is also the ominous new power of the Church that has emerged on the Polish political scene, which many in Poland find difficult to reject because of its radicalising role during the years of oppression.

Stories from Romania come from a single school in a deprived part of Bucharest. They were the result of the teacher's assignment to the class, suggested by a Romanian friend in London with whom I was in touch. They capture the deprivations, the heroisms. The Romanian contributors were the youngest – at the time of the revolution some were only eleven or twelve years old – but without any doubt they are the bravest. They met face to face with death. Their revolution was raw, cruel and as fast as lightning.

And the three Soviet stories from Moscow? They came hot from the writers' pens, delivered by another friend, Pieta, who went to Moscow for a few days. I was so glad that they could be included: they square the whole collection. They talk of the events of August 1991, the aborted communist coup against Gorbachev. And though the accounts centre on a few days, their significance is clear. There is the end of the dying monster, the last breath of the old dictatorship. All the East Europeans were waiting for the giant to move, to stop strangling them. It gave them the freedom to have their own revolutions and Gorbachev for some time became the hero of the people of Berlin and Prague when people took to the streets and marched in demonstrations against their own ageing dictators. They called: 'Gorby, come and see what is happening here', as the East European governments in their mortal fear tightened their last grip over populations. I remember a friend in Prague telling me that to watch Soviet TV became an exciting pastime after years and years of having to digest the boring Soviet drama of boring Soviet tractor drivers riding victoriously into the communist sunset. This used to be the compulsory viewing. Now, Gorby represented something different. Yet the Soviet Union didn't move beyond its top-down initiated *perestroika*. The aborted coup changed that. It achieved, for at least a short time, the opposite of what it intended to achieve: it united and politicised the people. How deeply this experience will go, only the generation of these young people can say. But the Soviet people were the last of the sleepy people in the old enclave of communist regimes. They have now woken up. The Soviet parliament suspended the Communist Party. It is the end of an era.

I don't think that there is any reason to gloat, however: not completely and not in the way western media often present this dramatic shift in world politics. Reading these stories, there are still numerous questions open, not least the one about what the west can offer with its declaration that democracy is a superior political system. These 'kids' have a very good instinct for lies. They have been surrounded by them for too long. They will not be fooled. They know that the transition will not be easy. They know that the so-called market economy has obvious flaws. They see it through their own eyes on their own streets now. There is poverty. They still somewhat stoically accept that some will win and some will lose. But on one thing they seem to be uncompromising: they will not stop asking new questions.

They watch the older generation groping for new truths. They know that some of them were the ones who kept the old system in motion, often unconsciously. They see that many of the new people are doing quite well now. A Prague couple at a tram stop quietly confided in each other: 'What do we have? Bloody dearer transport that doesn't come, whilst the guys in the town hall ride for free!'

The past has its continuities. It can't be swept clean away in one stroke. This is what these young people know and express so well. It's evident to them that changing the people at the top is not the solution. New or recycled 'old boys' networks' have sprung up; intolerance, old scores, getting rich quick, all come into play. Could one agree that 'There are no democrats in many parts of Eastern Europe, only anti-communists?' And who are the anti-communists? The questions multiply. A friend of my generation told me: 'There is a little sleeping apparatchik in all of us. It can't be otherwise.' The shock of realising it came to me when I was driving through the peaceful Czech countryside and stopped at a tiny local petrol station. Another car pulled up next to me. The driver jumped out, wasting no time, and screamed at me: 'You came the wrong way in! This is a one-way entry. You broke the law! I'll call the police!' I stood there silently and shook my head. Yes, the damage of the past forty years goes deeper than the collapsed economy, the neglect of buildings and the environment. I would not be exaggerating if I said that had I defended myself I would not have been taken seriously, least of all because I am a woman.

But the book is also full of real hopes and new openings. I feel that I have nothing more to say. The stories speak for themselves. Though they are a truly random and haphazard collection, it is in the best of East European fashion. My only decision was on how to arrange them. There was the possibility of following the chronology of the countries' recent political histories:

Hungary was the first to liberalise: it never 'needed' a revolution. It was always seen as the 'most cheerful barracks of Eastern Europe'. The young Hungarians feel self-possessed, sometimes sure of their country's advantages, sometimes worried about the political danger of its openness. But for them it was the political present that was important.

Poland, although the first to have a non-communist government, never had as smooth a ride as Hungary. The drama of martial law, when its own army went against the people is still very much at the back of people's minds. It's a country that was once seen as the most radical. Will the new system stifle that completely?

East Germany made headlines when masses of East Germans crossed the borders through Hungary and then Czechoslovakia. They fled. There was rupture, there was the storming of the Berlin Wall. How can these young people feel settled? Now it's the Deutschmark that rules their lives.

Czechoslovakia followed. It was at one stage totally unpredictable. It had a staunchly hardline government. It was the young people who acted. They were given the credit in 1989 – but now?

Romania is best remembered for its uncompromising stand towards its own dictator, Ceaucescu, who was executed within days of the popular unrest. The speed of events, the lack of broader participation perhaps shows now. The country is suffering, many confusions remain, the hardship continues.

The Soviet Union, as I mentioned, is a chapter of its own. A backward-going history, the new awakening. Now, no more.

After some deliberations, the Romanian stories were chosen to come first. Through the youngest eyes one is brought right into the heart of the events. These stories are followed by East Germany, Czechoslovakia, Poland, Hungary and The Soviet Union. There will be plenty of historical chronologies and studies. This is the first private viewing . . .

But other countries of what was the East European bloc have been left out. Not because of our lack of interest; we simply did not have enough contacts. I would like to apologise for that. These countries are not forgotten. Especially Yugoslavia, which is going through the trauma of years of accumulated wrong policies, the pretence of liberalism under the western label of federalism. There are problems that go deep into its history and the history of the whole region. Frustrated political forces on both sides are trying to settle scores that are not of ordinary people's making. The wrongdoings of rigid communism meet with the wrongdoings of often Fascist-inspired nationalism.

The peoples of Eastern Europe have been divided from each other, their lives fragmented. They were kept apart by fear, and then artificially glued together under one giant political system. Their diversity, their original richness, their love of life, and their new fears appear in the pages of these stories. I want to express my thanks to the contributors once more. For the time being I shall try to ignore my daughter's sobering words to me: 'You would be interested in Eastern Europe, wouldn't you!', and hope that the reading will be enjoyable both for those who know Eastern Europe and for those who want to find out.

ROMANIA

Romania was rightly regarded as the most oppressed of the countries of Eastern Europe. The seeming liberalism of Ceaucescu's international politics when he refused to back up the Soviet-led invasion of Czechoslovakia in 1968 rested on a very hardline domestic policy. His policies grew increasingly autocratic, it was a true one-man dictatorship with family members employed as ministers, military chiefs and judges. The country suffered. To pay off foreign debts, food was exported that was otherwise unavailable at home. To catch up with the developed nations, large-scale industrialisation took place, displacing villages and creating one of the worst areas of environmental pollution in central Europe. Ethnic minorities were mistreated. Women were mistreated. It became illegal to obtain any contraception: to reproduce became a patriotic duty. The state banned abortions. In December 1989, it all exploded. It started in the Hungarian minority enclave of Timisoara. Ceaucescu and his wife Elena were executed on Christmas Eve and a new government of National Salvation emerged. Things, unfortunately, hardly changed. The people suffer still. There is no food. Securitate, the secret police, simply regrouped and the present government is full of old personalities. There was an exodus of German and Hungarian minorities. There is anti-Semitism. The price of petrol has doubled. There are 24-hour queues. In December 1990 Timisoara called a virtual general strike, calling for the resignation of the President and regional police chiefs. Strikes continue. The former King Michael tried to enter Romania, was first expelled, then his citizenship was restored. Miners came to the capital with clubs, smashing some of the governmental buildings. They were not to be used by Iliescu's New Salvation Front government again. The people are angry. It's time for the 'second Romanian revolution', they say.

Population: 22.8 million
Capital: Bucharest

1878 – Declaration of independence from the Turks; remains a kingdom.
1918 – New territories such as Transylvania added after the end of the First World War.
1930s – A Fascist dicatorship, first royal then military.
1940 – Abdication of King Carol II; Transylvania transferred to Hungarian rule.
1941 – Support given to Hitler's invasion of the Soviet Union.
1944 – Red Army reaches Bucharest in August.
1946 – National Democratic Front government in power, which brings about a reign of terror.
1947 – King Michael abdicates; Paris Peace treaty restores Transylvania to Romania; the country is declared a People's Republic.
1948 – Merger of the Communist Party and Social Democrats forming the Romanian Workers' Party, which follows a rigid Stalinist line; nationalisation and

collectivisation; ruthless treatment of the peasantry.
1964 – Declaration of the Communist Party's sovereignty.
1965 – Ceaucescu comes to power; change of name to Socialist Republic; elimination of opposition; Ceaucescu's family members promoted to top posts.
1968 – Refuses to take part in the Warsaw Pact invasion of Czechoslovakia.
1970s – Accelerated large-scale industrialisation.
1972 – Joins IMF and the World Bank to take up loans.
1984 – Ceaucescu has total control, holds posts of President of the Republic and of the State Council, Secretary-General of the Communist Party, Head of Executive Committee, of the Defence Council, etc.
1989 – Romanian revolution; execution of Ceaucescu and his wife Elena in December; country run by the National Salvation Front with Iliescu and Roman.
1990 – Spate of strikes against the present government.

Magdalena Sava, aged 13, Bucharest
MY BRAVE FATHER

I'm a girl in class VII from number 113 school in Bucharest. Though it happened a year and three months ago, I remember every moment and every second of the revolution. That 'hot' holiday I was due to go to my mother's relatives in the Calarase district, but I remained in Bucharest because of family problems. But since I don't like staying at home during holidays, I went to spend time at my grandmother's, who also lives in the capital. I like it there: my parents came almost every evening and we listened to radio Free Europe, which told us about the uprising in Timisoara; that was how we found out about the massacres there. We couldn't believe it. But on 21 December my grandmother came back from work and told us about Ceaucescu's meeting and the turn of events. This was confirmed when we saw the TV images and the tyrant's face contorted with fear.

Then started in our house the white nights and days glued to the telly. My grandpa who works in the oxygen station of a big hospital was on night shifts. There, they were shooting all the time. The three soldiers who were guarding the oxygen room were from the so-called 'works unit' and couldn't even handle a gun. My grandpa taught them how to shoot and they were as diligent as new pupils.

My father went to work, to guard the thermoelectric station with his colleagues. My father was very brave until one night when a big tracer bullet fell into the station yard – they all panicked and thought their end had come! When it happened a second time, however, they knew it was just a 'con', shrugged their shoulders and said: 'God is with us.'

I myself meant nothing to the revolution, I just stayed in the warmth at home, but other children my age were in the streets. I was thinking about victory and was making plans for the future: it will be better, with better TV, culture to be savoured to the full, children will learn more, lies will not exist, there'll be *freedom*.

Ciobanu Oana, aged 13, Bucharest
OUR HEROES

I am one of the thousands of children living in Bucharest, who took part in something not many children will live through from now on. I am the redhead from the seventh D form of school number 113, sector 4.

I was at my grandparents' when the revolution started. I was playing in the yard when I heard announcements made time and time again on the radio. They appealed to everyone to come and defend the achievements of the revolution. I was petrified, I didn't realise what was happening, but everything became clear when I watched the TV broadcast. Immediately my thoughts turned to my father who had remained in Bucharest: I knew he wasn't just standing with his arms crossed, and I was to be proven right. During those moments my father was on the streets of the city, along with thousands of revolutionaries. I was watching TV with my grandparents, who were crying with joy, hoping that we, the young generation would have a better life than our parents had. I envied my neighbours who had remained in Bucharest, thinking how proud they must be to be able to participate directly in the shaping of our people's future, that was being tested so hard during those days. I was shaken by the way those bad men had destroyed the National Art Museum with all that was in it and the Central Library that contained our people's whole spiritual wealth accumulated over the years. I was very much impressed by the images from the Palace Place.

My God! There was a sea of people. I couldn't believe my

eyes – there were so many people united by the same wish: to topple the dictator. Many tried to stop them, but to no avail, their time had come. Through the revolution I became acquainted with the feeling of hatred, hatred towards those who had killed innocent children, women and men. I have a feeling of veneration for those who gave their lives so that the future of our country could be changed.

Each winter, when Christmas comes, we will remember that one Christmas full of bloodshed that obliges us, who are alive, to go on fighting for those ideals.

Nica Dan, aged 12, Bucharest
MEMORIES OF THE REVOLUTION

I am a twelve-year-old boy, a pupil in the seventh form.

I spent my winter holidays at home with my parents. I used to play football with my friends every day, on the playground at the back of our block of flats and afterwards we would rest.

One of those days, while I was chatting with my friends, we noticed that the people on the streets were very excited, they were stopping in groups. Some were happy, others, especially the women, were scared. We approached one group. What had happened? It was the revolution.

For us it was something that had never ever happened before and we were extremely curious. We followed all the events on TV. It was as if we had taken part in the revolution itself, through television. It was extraordinary and moving.

But it wasn't only watching TV that aroused our emotions, events were also taking place in and around our flats.

The flat where I live is right across from an army barracks. This military unit has been, throughout the revolution, a regular nest of firecrackers.

Because of its position, the terrace on our block of flats was the best place to survey the barracks. This was why they put two rifles in position up there, and two strong floodlights as well and about half a dozen soldiers. The entrance to the house was also being guarded by two or three soldiers, who watched each staircase. Of course people living in the flats took care of the soldiers and brought them food and hot coffee.

During one of the evenings, around ten o'clock, a jeep stopped in front of the barracks, trying to get in. Four men got out of the jeep. The soldiers on guard noticed that the four had arms hidden under their coats. Then hell broke loose. There was shooting from the barracks, and the four men were shooting too.

The night was shredded by the light arrows of the bullets. After the shooting had stopped, the car and the four men were destroyed. And there were other events of that kind that scared tenants stiff.

But in spite of it all, the people stuck with the soldiers.

Watching the revolution on TV I was impressed by the people's courage and sense of unity.

I kept thinking: something marvellous is happening, something that very rarely occurs. I was impressed by the men, by the hard look in their eyes. During all that time I never gave a thought to what would happen afterwards.

But now I wish that I and the other children of my age will have a better life, and a wealthier one, than our parents and our grandparents have had.

Bugeanu Anca, aged 13, Bucharest
BLOODSTAINED DECEMBER

I am one of thousands of children who had the chance to witness something really extraordinary. Although time wipes the blackboard of memory like a sponge, the events of December 1989 have remained deeply etched into my memory. Then I was only twelve years old and didn't understand fully what was happening. For me, everything started on the morning of the 22nd, while I was looking out of the window of the dining room. Something strange was in the air, something that made it hard to breathe. And there was something else – there were no children outside. Why? I would have the answer in a couple of hours. From time to time I could see groups of workers who had come out of the factories. Why? The shifts hadn't ended yet; it was only twelve o'clock. And there was a noise – a horrible rumbling noise that made you feel very strange: a mixture of fear and ignorance. All these thoughts and feelings mingled in my brain haphazardly. I didn't understand a thing and had no one to ask, as I was alone, so I started to read. I can even remember what I was reading. Just a commonplace book of fairy-tales, a book telling of beautiful days full of sunshine, with crystal-clear blue skies. I was caught up in those lines full of beauty when the shrill sound of the doorbell woke me from my reveries. It was my best friend, Alina. She had come to call me to her place because she was alone at home, and afraid. Afraid? Afraid of what? I asked her.

'What? Don't you know, then? I saw the tanks passing.'

'Tanks? In Bucharest? What did they look like?'

I was to see for myself those compact iron-heaps, meant to inspire fear. Fear. It was the word you could hear everywhere you went. Although nobody said it out loud, it was in all the mysterious cracks of things. It was the word that was to conquer the whole city.

When we reached Ali's place we turned on the radio, hoping to hear something to brighten us up. But what we got was troubled waters. We heard repeated appeals. In the meantime, my mother came, and we asked her to explain what was happening. She was the one who told us about the revolution. Mother went home and left me with Alina. She told us to be good, not to look out of the window and not to open the door to anyone.

So there was a revolution: a revolution like those in the history books, with many pictures. Alina's parents still didn't come, but the deafening noise that followed made us forget everything. Then I saw a real tank. We went down to my place. Mother was watching TV. We thought it was a detective story: bullets were flying over the buildings and people were dying. But who was doing the shooting? It was probably the police shooting at the drug-dealers. Still, the buildings looked familiar. Yes, it was actually the Television Building. Then ... it wasn't a movie, after all – this was really happening. When did it take place? I knew of no revolution during the last thirty years in Romania. It could only mean that what we saw was happening then and there.

How much it had taken for me to understand it all. And father was out, he was attending a meeting. That meant ... that he was probably there. Father? Never. What if ...? But that couldn't be.

He came home soon enough. He had really seen it all. He told us about things we could hardly imagine. Then our attention was once again attracted by the TV. There were desperate appeals again, asking people to come out and fight. The TV set was my link to the revolution: the first Romanian revolution to be broadcast live.

As nothing goes on for ever, it came to an end. Everything came to an end. But it was a shocking end – thousands of people dead, who would never come back to receive our gratitude, the gratitude of the living. Dozens of buildings destroyed. The first time I went out again was two weeks later, accompanied by my parents, of course, to see the horrible aftermath for ourselves.

It was a real disaster. We went to the Cemetery of the Heroes of the Revolution, the cemetery of the heroes of immortality. It was full of marble crosses, as white as milk, a pure white, like the tears of the mothers grieving the loss of their sons and daughters.

Today is 13 March, an ordinary day, still it is different from the March days of the past in that it is the first 13 March in liberty.

A new world is being built. A better one, it has to be better.

That holy December, red with innocent blood, will be for ever on my mind, surrounded by a halo of light.

Petrică Răzvan, aged 13, Bucharest

IMPRESSIONS OF THE REVOLUTION

My name is Petrică Răzvan and I am a child of Bucharest, the town that has been through so much during the last two years. We learned about revolutions in history, but we never knew what that really meant. But alas we have lived through the real lesson of history that has toppled the communist regime. It all started on 22 December 1989.

I knew that mother had left in the morning to attend some courses, and father was in Italy. I was alone at home. Suddenly I heard people in the streets shouting slogans against communism and Ceaucescu. I ran towards the window and saw a huge column approaching: people were marching towards the town. The rows of people seemed endless. They were shouting 'Come with us!', they were firm, with harsh faces and clenched fists. I realised then that Ceaucescu was bound to fall and that people were going to die for that. I was scared and I started to cry. I was so alone and I was thinking: where is my mother? I turned on the TV and watched the first images of the revolution in amazement. Late at night, when the shooting had already started at the Palace Place, mother came back. She told me she was coming from the Palace Place and that the two tyrants had fled. Later on my father arrived, via Timisoara. He had seen some scenes from the revolution taking place there. After the revolution I felt really free.

Macaşoi Marius, aged 13, Bucharest
THE REVOLUTION ON 22 DECEMBER 1989

I waited impatiently for the winter holidays. My father and I were going to stay with my grandparents, to see some customs from the Puieni village in Giurgiu.

At my grandparents' I was walking down the street with my aunt when I heard the radio in a neighbour's yard. It said a revolution had begun ...

I ran to my grandparents' place immediately and turned on the radio. We all sat on the porch, listening. We started to cry, worrying about mother who was alone in Bucharest.

Father went to Bucharest to look after mother. But she wasn't at home: a neighbour told him she had gone to Olteniţa.

In the meantime, we in the countryside didn't know what had really happened in Bucharest and in the other important towns, but we became more and more interested by what we heard on the radio. My uncles and my grandparents were quite worried about my cousin, who was in the army. In the evening we sat on the porch looking at how the starry sky was lit up. We heard the shooting at Mihai Bravu.

Father returned home on 25 December 1989, and my sister and I came home one day before the beginning of the new term. Mother starting telling us how she could hear the bullets, how she cried while she was watching TV and how she fell asleep every night, full of fear.

We were very sad about the many people who had died in the revolution, the many children who had become orphans and the many parents who had lost their children. I felt an ice-cold shiver. These people deserve to be called heroes because they gave their lives for our freedom.

Codîrleanu Cristina, aged 13, Bucharest

IN LOVE WITH FREEDOM

I am just an ordinary girl, a pupil of the seventh form and I go to school number 133.

When the revolution started I was staying with my grandparents. One day, as I was watching TV, I became aware of the revolution. On the streets of the village people were talking about the revolution. I couldn't take part in any of the events, because in the village of Făcăeni, in the county of Ialomița there wasn't the turmoil of Bucharest, Timisoara, Sibiu and other places. Watching the revolution and the tanks on TV and listening to people talk about it I was shocked. There were many children my age, some older, some even younger and many old people: people without their clothes, attacked with rifle bullets, without fear of death, children waving flags and dying with no regret in the revolution for *freedom*.

Before I had found out about the revolution, in the countryside where my grandparents live some men, the 'terrorists', had set fire to the hay people fed the cattle with. There were policemen on every street to protect the hay and to see who was setting it on fire. One evening, about half-past ten, an old man came down the street with a shovel on his shoulder. The policemen took him to the station and asked him what he was doing on the streets at that hour. He answered that he had been working. Afterwards they bound him and beat him up and kept asking him where he had been, although this man was innocent.

My wish for my future and that of the children of my age is: 'let there be a better and more beautiful world.'

Gârgău Maria, aged 13, Bucharest

COMPOSITION WITHOUT A TITLE, *or* DISCOVERY

A day like all the others. Warm but not very. It was winter, after all: the 17th or 18th.
I was in a white car with my parents and my sister, passing by the Military Academy. The place was familiar, because we bought our gas nearby. I noticed something unusual: the soldiers were wearing war helmets. We – my family, that is – knew nothing of what was going on in Timisoara. We had been away, in the provinces. There were some explanations, but none could satisfy me. Next day we found out what had happened in the country.
Of course, the meeting organised by comrade Ceaucescu followed on 21 December. My mother happened to read in a newspaper about the film and theatre performances of that day. Without much ado, we decided to go to a movie in a cinema near the Central Committee's building. We had turned off the TV – the meeting was going ahead as planned. We were dressed and ready to go. Luck was on our side, for I was quarrelling with my sister about whether we should go by car or by tube. All of a sudden we heard whistling on the radio. With a speed totally unexpected of her, my mother turned on the TV. But all we saw was 'live transmission' written across the screen and the music to go with it was 'patriotic songs'. The images came back, but the people no longer held slogans and photographs, only flags.
When father came home he told us: 'The people were tightly packed together in a mass whose noise was deafen-

ing, a sound of terror and death. You couldn't resist the wave without risking being trodden underfoot. Fear of death turned people into beasts. One could have done anything, even killed, to get away. I walked home for safety.'

We could hear the tanks driving down Olteniţei Highway. The children playing behind the block of flats rushed into their homes. We knew there was an army barracks nearby. At that time my grandfather was in the Vitan-Bîrzeşti hospital, near the barracks. He was very happy that we were free. He died shortly afterwards; he had no more time to live. There was a night of terror, with bullets lighting up the sky, and we could hear rifles bellowing as far away as the police headquarters. And I know for sure that there was even the thunder of cannons.

I was completely bewildered. On 22 December when I found out that the party secretary had fled I had a powerful shock, which turned everything I had known upside down. On TV I saw rows of fire hitting the building of the Central Committee and those who were around it. I had the impression I was watching a movie. If I hadn't heard the bullets nearby I still wouldn't have believed it was true.

It was only then that I realised how far away I am from this world. I realised that I live in my thoughts anywhere other than on earth. For me life and death don't exist, I feel the presence of the living and the dead alike. Even if I can't perceive them all by smell, by sight or by hearing, there still is this sensation of closeness, of unreality, that I can't get rid of. In any case, hospital number 9, for mental diseases, is close by.

I wait to see what will happen, but in my family everything has remained unchanged. The only difference is that we are more irritable, much more irritable than before.

Dina Adriana, aged 13, Bucharest
AN END COVERED IN BLOOD

The doorbell rang for a long time. I stood up and went to open the door. It's only nine o'clock, I thought, looking at my watch in amazement.

I came into the dining room. The hour was the same as on that hot 22 December when I, a mere child of twelve who had never known the hardships of life because of my parents who did everything for me, was running towards the windows of the dining room, drawn by the typical curiosity of children, triggered by a horribly strange and morbid rumbling. I wanted the windows to disclose the mystery of that sinister sound that was impregnating every fibre of my body with a new sensation, a mixture of anxiety and fear.

I stood transfixed, with my eyes on the vehicles producing that hellish noise: tanks. It was the first time that I had laid eyes on those steel colossi, made only to spread death and tears.

With difficulty bits of reality started coming back to me. Yes, father had mentioned something last night about some groups of demonstrators. But I couldn't link the groups of people to those columns of tanks and trucks full of soldiers from the neighbouring barracks. But weren't these vehicles of death sent against those people my father had told me about? No, that was impossible. The thought sent a dreadful shiver down my spine.

There was no one to enlighten me; my parents had gone to see my grandparents. After a couple of seconds I looked around more attentively. Now I really couldn't understand anything at all. The nearby windows and balconies were full of people throwing flowers and encouraging those who were passing by. Soon the pavements were invaded by an enthusiastic crowd. Seeing this I asked myself in bewilderment: 'Where do all these people come from? It's Friday, and they should be at work until the evening.'

I simply didn't understand anything. What happened was beyond my powers of understanding.

As I was on holiday and had nothing much to do anyway, I turned on the TV to watch one of the programmes from the neighbouring countries. I was surprised that Romanian television was broadcasting at that hour. Finally it dawned on me that something important was happening. I found out soon enough what it was, by the presenter's announcements. Then I went out. Groups of people who were talking excitedly confirmed and at the same time strengthened the things I had heard on TV: a revolution of the Romanian people had truly begun. A revolution that would redden and heat up that end of December, making it glow for ever in the memory of each person who lived through those dreadful days.

I went back home and from then on the TV wasn't turned off for two whole days.

We were following each news item, each detail. In front of my eyes I saw people I knew, and some I didn't, on whose faces I could read concern and who asked the population to come and defend the radio and TV buildings. There were also images from the streets of Bucharest. The impression was of watching a horror movie. Crowds of people, gathered in different places, surrounded by buildings; from their tops death was flying in an outburst of shouts, sighs and shots. It left pools of blood behind, and those we can't thank today for everything that they offered to us. It was all real, then. All those tens of thousands of people who were alive, only a couple of minutes ago. Perhaps they were making plans for the future: it only took a second to change the smile on their face into the cry of death.

Evening came. I was thinking worriedly about mother and father (there was no room for other thoughts). Why hadn't they come back yet? I have never expected them more anxiously. I was wondering whether they would be able to get through the places where death was taking its toll. At last they came. Everything was over in a couple of days, but the whole country was crying. Crying because of the joy it had won through the sacrifice of the beloved ones, crying in the places where the marble monuments of their sons would be built.

The insistent doorbell woke me from my reverie. I finally went to open the door.

Alina Roşca-Stănescu, aged 13, Bucharest

THINGS THAT SHOULDN'T BE FORGOTTEN

It was about six o'clock in the morning when my father barged into the bedroom like a storm. He had received a phone call from Timisoara, bringing happiness but also concern. It's easy to understand why.

Ever since that day our house practically turned into a small news agency. As soon as we received another call from Timisoara we would ring up dozens of friends, 'reporting' the latest news. Other friends came by and we told them what else had been going on, and they, in their turn, told others.

When the so-called revolution began in Bucharest too, everybody was elated with happiness, embracing everyone else, hopping with joy and singing out loud. I had double reason to rejoice because no one asked me to do my homework.

But the first outburst was soon brutally stopped by the deaths of many young people and other demonstrators.

From now on, everything I know I know from my parents and my friends.

The beginning – that outburst of songs and sincerity – united the people and made them capable of a marvellous thing – they were able to forgive. The soldiers and the police with shields were covered with flowers and treated with understanding. Many of the soldiers befriended the revolutionaries. It was clear that they would never have shot at the population. But an unforeseen thing happened, which my father noticed, and that helped him during the first moments of confusion. The soldiers were changed; it isn't known who else came instead, dressed the same way. Many people died then, but the way their bodies were defiled was just as dreadful. There was not much difference, actually, in the way the wounded and the corpses were treated. A neighbour told us about that, a very kind and honest person. He was covered with blood: he had carried the dead, fighting for them, because there had been a real fight between the Securitate agents who wanted the corpses in order to burn them and to cover up all the traces, and the people who wanted the dead to have a burial. Agents in black overalls entered the Colţea hospital by force and killed many of the wounded.

In the mean time, about ten o'clock, the workers succeeded in getting out of the factories and they gathered in the Palace Place. Then Ceaucescu fled in his helicopter.

When the revolution was at its height, Ion Iliescu appeared, acting like a national hero. I will end this description with a fact that may throw light on its outcome. In the evening of 22 December Iliescu was speaking without any disturbance whatsoever from the palace balcony, which was lit by floodlights. As long as he was speaking, nobody fired a shot. But shortly afterwards grim bullets claimed the lives of the people who had gathered to celebrate their victory, but without hitting anyone on the balcony.

GERMANY

East Germany is no more. It has been 'taken over', as most people admit. It has always been a country of split identities, often of split families. Its politics was a complicated compromise between being a 'shop window' to the West, trying to prove to the world that communism works, and keeping a very rigid and grim Stalinist hold over people. So it is inevitable that the previous division of the two Germanies, and their unification since October 1990, forms a centrepiece in people's ways of thinking.

Since 1982–3 there has been a series of protests in East Germany, the Lutheran Church becoming a pillar of support and of contact with the outside world. Peace demonstrations and anti-NATO demonstrations followed. Since 1984, there had been greater contact with West Germany and officially some emigration was allowed.

October 1989 was the date of the official celebration of forty years of communism, attended by Gorbachev, who watched the popular protest that followed. It is rumoured that he came to trigger Soviet-style *perestroika* in East Germany and was not very sympathetic to Honecker who had been the East German leader for almost twenty years. Another rumour has it that Honecker, Ceaucescu of Romania and Jakeš of

Czechoslovakia, the hardline trio, were plotting an anti-Gorbachev move. The disrupted celebrations, with no offer of help from Gorbachev, turned into a mass exodus of East Germans into the West. First through Hungary, then Czechoslovakia, there were 300,000 of those who said no to Honecker's communism. He resigned, Krenz took over, legalised the New Forum, the main oppositional group, and lifted all travel restrictions: the Berlin Wall came down. Honecker fled to Moscow. By October the following year, 1990, Germany was reunified. Not without protests and acrimony, though. First against Stasi, the secret police, then against the dropping of all the welfare provisions that East Germany had enjoyed. There is 30 per cent unemployment in some parts, and the rise of neo-Nazism, with attacks on foreign *émigrés* in particular, is deeply disconcerting to everyone.

Population: 16.7 million
Capital: East Berlin

1945 – Germany divided into four occupation zones held by the allied forces: US, Britain, France and the USSR.
1949 – Foundation of the German Democratic Republic in the Soviet zone.
1953 – Industrial workers' uprisings in East Berlin and other cities.
1961 – Creation of the Berlin Wall in August; East Germany's borders are sealed.
1971 – Ulbricht, leader of the East German Communist Party for over twenty years, replaced by Honecker.
1972 – A basic treaty signed with West Germany to promote trade and later informal diplomatic contacts.
1975 – A new treaty signed with the Soviet Union to reinforce East Germany's loyalty to the Soviet bloc.

1984 – Culmination of protests of pro-peace and anti-NATO demonstrations.
1988 – Calls for removal of Berlin Wall from 5,000 people who listen to rock concert on the other side of the wall; radical demands put through the Church challenging the party.
1989 – East German exodus to the West; creation of the New Forum, a main dissident movement. November – storming of the Berlin Wall. Honecker leaves for Moscow.
1990 – Unification of the two Germanies, following their monetary union. 48% voted Christian Democrats.

FROM THE MAGAZINE
MENSCHENSKINDER

Monika Weber, aged 17, Goslar
Brother?

In the beginning was the
Opening of the borders,
Jubilation, tears of joy, laughter,
Brother.

Then came the Trabbis [Trabants]
And the 'we greet you money',
Jealousy, envy, hatred
Shit 'Ossi' [Easterner]!

Now unity shall come,
Scepticism, mistrust, egoism,
Brother?

Stefan Schwalbe, aged 14, Berlin, East Germany
By the Grave

Sunday

The Wall is open. I shall not see my great-aunt. Ever! She is dead. Two months ago she was still alive. I stand in the graveyard, by her grave. I have never seen her, but I knew she was waiting for me . . . Around me all is white. She waits for me again. I shall see her . . . some time in a better world.

On Monday Mike comes to me and says: 'If the Wall had been opened two months earlier, I could have gone to the Metallica concert.'

Deike Busing, aged 11, Obernburg

Surely, all German citizens want reunification, but have we asked if the DDR [East Germany] wants it? This might sound absurd, but surely it is a fact that not only the BRD will have to pay. One may speak out against the DDR and their former system as much as one likes, but in many ways they were ahead of us, starting with nursery places (which are still a lucky catch here) to the crèches for children of working mothers (men in the BRD should consider whether they give women with children the chance to work).

I personally think that the good we could learn from the DDR is going to be destroyed in a 'lightning reunification'. But we carry on regardless, hoping that things do work out and we end up all-knowing big heads on the winning side.

The BRD leads, the DDR follows – that is how things have progressed so far (and not much has happened in spite of all the haste!)

Of course the DDR has a lot to learn, but we must not get blunted. Sometimes I think things will have to go very wrong again before we understand.

W., aged 18, East Germany
A Missed Opportunity

I love my country. Formerly I doubted it, but now as I am losing it, I notice how attached I am to it. We are losing a chance which is not likely to recur, to build an alternative to all dictatorial systems (e.g. Stalinism, capitalism). Unfortunately, people here make decisions according to their gut feelings, instead of listening to their hearts and minds.

W., aged 19, West Germany

Actually, I don't like Germany, but I do notice that when I am in a foreign country and someone calls me names because I am German, then I defend Germany. In many ways Germany is only the smallest of all evils . . .

W., aged 18, East Germany
Not a Bit More Moral!

Capitalism is not a bit more moral! Quite the contrary. Socialism did not work, but the basis of capitalism – namely, that which makes money is good – is a deeply odd and amoral one. However, what I like about your moderate capitalism – and after all it's all decided now – is the relative freedom allowed with relation to non-fundamental issues, which means there are niches or slots for alternative viewpoints.

W., aged 17, West Germany

First of all I used to feel really fed up about DDR citizens, who were allowed to park anywhere without a fine, who cashed their 'we greet you money' and polluted the air with their 'Trabbi' cars. I live on the border zone and it was particularly bad here. The 'poor' DDR citizens were simply allowed to do anything and everybody felt sorry for them. I am rather sceptical about this 'lightning reunification' – it was too hurried, too quick.

Katja Kriewitz, aged 18, Magdeburg
(East Germany)
Their Own Fault?

As a young person, I am particularly enjoying the changes which have happened here in the DDR. At least we can speak freely, vote freely, and travel – all things which we were prevented from doing. So I resent the remarks of those who have had this freedom all the time, who are afraid of losing something because of us, or of having to sacrifice something because of us; and those who regard us as second-class citizens, regarding us as being fully responsible for this complete disaster (although I have my reservations about it being a complete disaster). I also resent those who see themselves as better than us, and who are in no way ready for co-operation – unfortunately.

From what I read about the DDR, the sort of things they want – the whole disaster is partly their own fault – makes me feel sick . . .

Well, well . . .

What Would You Like to Call the New Germany?

Youth from DDR: McKohl-Country, don't know but the word *deutsch* shouldn't be in it.

Youth from BRD: Ecological-Social Republic of Germany, Federation of Germany.

I am not keen on reunification, but it will come. One can only make the best of it. However, nothing could persuade me to live in a Germany of that sort.

Simone Schein, aged 18, Chemnitz, East Germany
Love for My Country?

I live in Chemnitz, in Saxony [Sachsen]. I can't claim to love Saxony. I probably know my way around here better than anybody else. What does it sound like when a person from Saxony speaks on television or on the radio? I believe it is the ugliest dialect in the whole of Germany. There are, of course, pretty things in Saxony, for instance the Elbsandstein mountains, but that is not why I love my homeland. We, the young people, don't really have any concept of what *Heimat* [homeland] means. I think there are many young people who think the same. I feel more comfortable here than I would living anywhere else, but that is because my friends and relatives live here. The real value attached to the concept of the 'mother country' has sunk to an all-time low under the regime. We were told to love and protect our homeland; but that was having to submit to the will of the Authorities rather than actually loving our country. We should learn to love our country and do something for it – we should save our environment! Those who don't will soon have no homeland to learn to love.

Angela Kunze, aged 27, Berlin
MY DIARY

The scene is Berlin, September 1989. I was just twenty-five years old and had decided to start studying theology after all. I only reached this decision after many 'detours'. When I was a child, I always wanted to join a circus and so I was trained to do acrobatics and gymnastics. However, once I had left school I learned a 'respectable' profession – I became a physiotherapist. Having finished my training, I worked for a year and a half in a Church-run hospital, before I was finally employed by East Germany's biggest private circus. After a year with the circus I moved to Berlin and worked as a freelance clown, without becoming state registered.

My parents brought my brothers and sisters and me up in a very open and unworried atmosphere. As vicar, my father had many ecumenical contacts across the borders of our country, so that even as a child I had already experienced a variety of people's backgrounds and points of view, and certainly more than was normally the case in a so-called socialist educational system. Accordingly I grew up privileged in a way, although my father was in prison for a time in 1961–3 for political reasons and our family was under state observation – so we had to live very simply.

By September 1986 I had moved to Berlin and was earning a living with casual work. I managed to build up a reputation as a pantomime performer and acrobat and was regularly employed by churches (play groups, youth clubs and church conferences) to do my own routine. As I was not a state-registered clown, I could not get any other public engagements. Nevertheless, it did allow me to be independent. Nobody controlled my work and I used this freedom to travel in Eastern Europe (often without a valid visa and with the help of some harmless hoodwinking). There I made contact with illegal Church and political groups in the CSSR (Czechoslovakia), Romania and Russia and helped to construct a network of solidarity. At the age of sixteen I was taken to the police for the first time for wearing the symbol of the Churches' Peace Movement in the DDR – the sign 'Swords into Ploughshares', and since then I have often been taken away and interrogated by the police. In the end I had to restrict my travels into Eastern Europe in order not to endanger the safety of others. Despite this, I was able to visit the west twice, on the second occasion as a member of the DDR Church Delegation to the West Berlin Kirchentag (Church Day) in June 1989.

Although seen from the outside it looked as if matters had improved in the DDR as far as trips to the west and democratisation were concerned, in reality the situation had worsened. Ceaucescu was presented by Honecker with a high-ranking medal, and our friendship with this brutal government was repeatedly brought to our attention. However, newspapers and films from the reformed socialist USSR were not permitted. Then, a few months later, in the spring of 1989 we had elections, but the ballot was obviously rigged and there was a wave of protest. Protest actions were carried out on the 7th of every subsequent month as a reminder of the original polling day, 7 May.

Everything came to a head with the news of events in Tiananmen Square on 2 June 1989. There was no doubt that the media supported the brutal repression of the 'counter-revolution'. As a protest against this attitude and out of a feeling of solidarity with the Chinese students, we met in our churches to pray and to demonstrate our concern – the so called *Mahnwachen* (Watchful Alert).

During the summer months the great exodus started, over the borders of Hungary to the west. Some of my friends and relatives left the country. I did not want to leave, believing rather in the need of opposition. I felt responsible for my country and hoped that reforms would be carried out throughout the entire socialist bloc. In September I had made contact with the 'New Forum' and was informed of the initiative to found an 'SPD' party in the DDR. However, I was not a member, nor had I signed any of their manifestos or joined any special group. At the beginning of October I wanted to go to Prague again, in order to arrange further contacts between groups in the DDR and CSSR, when suddenly, the frontier to the CSSR was closed. On that day, 3 October 1989, a new era in my life began, which was to have a profound effect upon me.

The following diary is not a conscious documentation of what happened, it is a part of my personal diary, which I have kept for several years. Nevertheless, what I wrote during those days in October 1989 was, without any deliberate effort on my part, a reflection of historical events.

Tuesday 3 October, at noon

My God! Things are getting out of hand now. A few minutes ago they announced that the Czechoslovakian borders have been closed. Since Sunday night, when 6,000 people were allowed to leave the Embassy in Prague, a further 4,500 people are seeking refuge, hoping to emigrate.

Yesterday a demonstration took place in Leipzig with about 15,000–20,000 people taking part. They had gathered after prayer in St Nikolei's Church. On Sunday we had a meeting here of the Democracy Now group, mainly theologists. The entire Alt Pankow district was out of bounds and there was a curfew and house arrests were made. Bishop

Forck was refused entry into the church by the Stasi [secret police].

All night tanks and rocket transporters rolled through town in preparation for the great military parade on Saturday. [Saturday 7 October is the date appointed to celebrate the 40th anniversary of the DDR.] I shall stay in Berlin for that day. The borders with Czechoslovakia are closed, so I won't be able to travel there anyway. Here there will be acts of protest, prayer, watches of exhortation, meetings, in short everybody will be on the alert.

Katharina plans to organise a prayer meeting in St Hedwig's Cathedral on Saturday.

Today I received more information at our preaching school about future protest action. News travels quickly. We are surrounded.

Tuesday 3 October, evening

I have made up my mind to do something which will change my life. Tomorrow I shall go on hunger strike in Gethsemane Church. I suppose it will be called 'Action-Fasting'. A decisive step for me. I have to realise this idea on my own. Hopefully my stomach won't give me trouble. I have never been without food for ten days (I want to fast for ten days to represent ten years of peace). There are always other people in the church – I won't be totally alone. Since 2 October there have been prayer watches in the church as a reminder of the illegal arrests in Leipzig and there is always a service at 6 p.m. in honour of the same cause. Well, if you don't eat, you don't need much sleep. I have talked to people about it. At last I am doing something! Katharina knows about it and is also enthusiastic.

We went to St Hedwig's Cathedral to see the vicar and arrange a special prayer meeting for 7 October. But it was a fruitless attempt, they were obviously afraid.

Next I approached Michael, who is the organiser for the prayer meetings in Gethsemane Church and also responsible for youth work. I also saw the vicar of the church. Then I went to Simon, and went with him (by bike, which was fun), to Bärbel Boley. Her flat was the centre for the New Forum, an organisation which I do not actually belong to. Rolf Heinrich was there and many other people, so I arranged to meet Bärbel on the following day. I wanted to discuss fasting, a solidarity fast or a hunger strike. For me as a Christian, a fast would be more suitable, but you can't put the state under pressure by simply fasting; perhaps it's going to have to be a hunger strike.

I know this is going to be something outrageous. However, I hope it will have some meaning. It is an action of solidarity.

In church I met Mathias and today, suddenly, Joachim stood in front of me. We had a good talk. Everybody is ready to talk now. People have opened up. Our sorrows and concerns make us feel close to each other. Now it is important to do the right thing.

Wednesday 4 October

Start of the day. It is nine o'clock. I have tidied the flat and packed my rucksack. I have attempted to write down my reasons for the fasting action in a few lines. Now I shall go to Bärbel and the church youth affairs office and then to Katharina. Next I must fetch my things and move into the church.

I had to promise the vicar that I will accept medical supervision and will ask Elfin about that. Lord, my God, bless my actions! Keep me from sin! Help prevent my being misused and strengthen my patience. My fasting started with the following proclamation:

FASTING ACTION
Positive action, non-violent resistance.
- I fast, to think and pray in tranquillity and abstinence and thus find a new direction for my life.
- I fast, to purify myself of fear and resignation, hatred and violence, impatience and sensation seeking.
- I fast, because I see no other way of expressing my opposition to our politicians who hypocritically celebrate the 40th anniversary of the DDR as their victory.
- I fast because, unlike the media, I am concerned about the great number of people who are leaving our country.
- I fast, in order to show solidarity with all people who believe in justice and suffer and are persecuted because of it.
- I fast, in the hope that others will come and join me (for hours, or days), so that together we may set an example and show our personal concern for this country and to show that we are ready to restrict our personal material needs for the cause.

Wednesday 4 October, 2 p.m.

An hour ago I went with Marianne to my flat to fetch my things. (Marianne works for the City Youth Concern and is now Minister for the Re-union 90.) I have had my proclamation typed and photocopied (1,000 copies). Neither Bärbel nor Marianne found fault with the wording. So far people approve of what I have written.

I am glad to be here in the church now. Whatever happens will be in God's hands. If I am fasting on my own, it will also be good. I did not see Katharina this morning to give her my latest news. When we arrived the church was guarded by the police. Marianne had to smuggle me and my belongings in through a side door.

Now since the proclamations have been handed out, I am not allowed to leave the church for security reasons, until my fast is ended.

Wednesday 4 October, 20.30 hours

So far it has been wonderful. We have had great conversations. I have been receiving praise from all sides and yet I feel encouraged rather than burdened by it. Just now it is quiet in the church; people approach, read my proclamation and then leave or remain a little while. I shall try to pray, to become tranquil inside. The conversations have had an agitating effect on me. Surely this is going to change. It is all so very exciting. It is good to do something like this for the first time and not to know how it is going to end.

Thursday 5 October, 7 a.m.

How marvellous to wake up under the high vaults of the church, a church lived in by people. I found it difficult to go to sleep, but I did not feel cold. Now, early in the morning it is really quiet. Yesterday, after my last diary entry, Katharina, Angelica and a friend came, so we could pray the *Komplet* together. Then Mathias came, bringing along a rather chaotic character who hopes to be a diplomat. We had a talk. Finally, Mathias played the organ for half an hour. It was half an hour after midnight and the organ music soothed me. I suppose I won't be able to join in so many conversations, but now it is still an important part of my fasting.

Today I have to guard against becoming the centre of interest. Again and again I have to review my reasons for this fast, to keep myself free of the corruption that all the commotion around me creates. Even so, in a few days' time these reasons I put down yesterday might feel far removed. I may discover something new while I am here.

Thursday 5 October, 11.15 hours

Talk amongst the DDR citizens here often centres around 7 October. Some people say that blood will flow in the streets. We are afraid. The thought that I am actually doing something now is a great help. There are others wanting to fast as well.

12.15 hours

I have just been approached with a request for an interview by a television team, in English, and I have offered my assistance. (So far I have had very little experience of the press. It never occurred to me that my action would attract the international press, who were already in Berlin for the events of 7 October.)

Again, conversations and really moving exchanges make this day memorable.

15.00 hours

One of the women who organises the vigils took pity on me and asked the photographers to stop. There were ten of them and after thirty minutes I was ready to crawl under my blanket. Soon the service will start and I have been asked to lead the singing.

1 a.m. at night

It seems a lot has happened. I am writing whilst Simon, Detlef and his friends are improvising their jazz concert in front of the altar.

It has been a trying day. There have been many interviews, the last being with Dutch television. During the service at least seven television teams were filming. The group of people fasting has grown. There were good things. Wolfram brought a fleece for me to lie on, and people brought flowers because they could not bring me food. Mathias played the organ and will play every day from Monday. Signs of solidarity!

There are now three of us fasting. One is a woman aged forty-one, called Ilona, who is a woodcarver. The other is a man around thirty who works at the zoo. He wants to stay until Saturday. Many people have put their names down, wishing to fast.

Friday 6 October, 17.00 hours

An unpleasant thing happened today. In the morning Brazilian television arrived and asked for some information. That was OK. Then someone from France arrived and took photos. Then Dutch television arrived. At first they just filmed. Then one of them started asking questions, having asked permission to broadcast what I said. At first they were sensible questions, but then he followed with some sensational political stuff. It was bad. Later Ilona complained bitterly that I had gone too far and acted like an exhibitionist. I was dumbfounded. Thank God Bettina and Sabine came to see me. Their visit was a comfort.

The situation in Dresden and Leipzig is serious. It looks more like civil war. What will happen to me, when I leave here? How can I find tranquillity with all this turbulence around me? Ilona's criticism was justified. I am trying to pray – so many people around me. I crawl under my blanket. My head is hot, my tongue burns, my stomach aches!

I hope the commotion around me will stop. Perhaps they will go elsewhere. But what will happen tomorrow?!

Saturday 7 October, 16.00 hours

After a beautifully calm morning we have experienced two hours of stressful interviewing with the media. I broke off an interview with the Hungarian television crew.

Two photographers came again today, although they had already taken lots of pictures yesterday. They greeted me in French but I did not recognise them and I responded tersely. I had been disappointed by the Hungarian team. After all, they are familiar with socialism and I expected understanding and not sensation seeking and superficial interest in spectacular remarks. The French supported and encouraged me. It is very difficult to remain balanced when in contact with representatives of the press, still at least there are good ones amongst them.

A journalist from New York sits here each day in a pew quietly for a while. He has told me he covered the protest marches with Martin Luther King back in the sixties and the events and atmosphere here reminded him of those days – but after all they are westerners.

21.15 hours

There was panic here an hour ago! Now all is quiet, there is a sense of shock. A songwriter sings songs by a Russian about the time of Stalin. Most of the people who are listening to him have come from the big demo in Alexander Square. They had been surrounded by police cordons and kept repeating in unison 'no force', 'New Forum', 'Gorbi', and kept singing the communist anthem. Many were captured and taken away by police, but the people resisted all violence. Then about 5,000 people entered our church, not knowing where to go. The police and Stasi were everywhere. We can hear the slogans, and now people rushing in are shouting, 'the bulls are after us'.

Saturday 7 October, 24.15 hours

Now the first influx of people into the church has come to a standstill. Bishop Forck has succeeded in getting permission from the police for people to leave in ones or twos quietly without getting arrested. Those who did not enter the church faced the police. It is rumoured that there were some ugly scenes. Until a little while ago the police had ringed the church armed with water cannons. People say that 5,000 demonstrators are on the way to the Gethsemane Church in Pankow. Everywhere people get out and on to the streets.

Sunday 8 October, 03.15 hours

Again more reports: around 6,000 people from Friedrichshain are on the way to this church. They will surely never arrive. An hour ago about a hundred people broke the police cordon and entered the church. We started public prayers. I was asked to lead the singing, but as I had just surfaced from deep sleep I was in no condition to do so. When people were allowed to voice their own intercessions, chaos broke out. People showed off over the microphone, told stories and shouted silly slogans. The mood became volatile. The press came and filmed and conducted interviews. Things started to get out of control. I talked with the deaconess about our presence here. She doubts that the church council will allow us to stay longer than 10 October. I hope we may stay until Friday in order to finish my ten days' fasting, or else I will have to find somewhere else.

Stephan, Thomas and others have told me that many people do not understand my action. I shall have to live with that.

(Sunday evening after the service the police again formed

a cordon around the church. The police did go too far. Hundreds of people were arrested, forced into lorries and vans and taken away. Some stayed for up to two days in police cells without anyone knowing their whereabouts. This brutal action against peaceful demonstrators and citizens shocked the people generally and caused a feeling of solidarity.)

Monday 9 October, 15.45 hours

People are arriving in droves, excited, shocked, crying and furious. If you start a discussion a group of people gathers straight away. Rolf Heinrich (New Forum) has come and speaks with the people.

Just a little while ago some children came in during an hour between lessons. They had watched the police battle yesterday in Schoenhauser Allee from their windows and were very excited.

Wolfgang arrived to pray with me, but there is no time or peace and quiet. A television team has arrived. I wonder how they got in!

The 'camp' of us 'fasters' looks romantic, especially where our young people sit. They are a bright point in much darkness. There are many candles, flowers, juice and other gifts people have brought in.

Physically, I feel no ill effects, only some loss of weight. I have no ailments and feel fully energetic. Ilona wants to fast continuously, so there will be people fasting even when I finish.

Today the church council will decide if we are allowed to stay. The vicar enquired if I am willing to help with the vigils after my fast. Daily, thousands of people arrive, but the burden of organisation, services and responsibility is borne by a handful of persons only.

17.45 hours

What a lovely surprise. A sister (deaconess) from Switzerland arrived to visit us. She knows me from Taize and she came with Conny and Peggy to assure me of their solidarity with us. I had a good talk with a Norwegian journalist, but we were interrupted many times. People have been coming to me in tears to talk about the events of yesterday. An old man bowed deeply and said that he had never missed a day's work in thirty years, but today in protest against so much injustice, he would stay in the church and not go to work.

Other people expressed similar sentiments of solidarity and confessed they had never been in a church in all their lives, but 'enough is enough' and they wanted to express their solidarity.

The church is chock-a-block already. Hopefully nothing will happen after the service. It could be dreadful.

19.15 hours

The service is in full swing. Each nook and cranny in the church is occupied. Jalda Rebling is singing, Bishop Forck is due to speak next. There are reputed to be thousands of people outside the church. In Leipzig everything is on the alert. A church has been equipped for use as an emergency hospital; only medical staff have passes to enter the town centre. The so-called Emergency First Aid Troupe has instructions to send all the wounded to prison hospitals!

So far all is peaceful here. But how will everything turn out eventually?

Tuesday 10 October, 10.00 hours

Everything went well yesterday. It turned out to be a festival of the people. After the service some people left the church, while others entered. The church stayed full. Outside crowds of people stood with swaying candles. All was peaceful and no police! News from Leipzig: 70,000 people crowded into the town centre and the police do not interfere. Today people enter a quiet church (at last a companion and I were able to pray quickly) and the talk is joyous, happy and hopeful. On the windowsills of all the houses round about candles have been lit. Thanks to an arrangement with Kurt Hasur it has been possible to offer an open dialogue in Leipzig!! Yesterday an almost euphoric mood reigned here when the news of talks came through. No grounds for joy yet. However, it is the first step in the right direction. For the first time today people do not exchange horrific news, but news of hope. But we have to watch out and be sober and ready to act decisively to remain on the right path.

Yesterday evening, Dr Uhlmann [a minister in the new government] came around at 22.00 hours and explained his ideas. The church was still more than full. Dr Uhlmann came late and people became restive. We therefore led with a hymn from our part of the church and everybody immediately quietened down. It was impressive how these masses of people sat down and became quiet. After the official talk, people were asked to put their questions over the microphone. Well, that idea misfired totally. People just showed off. A mentally deranged person started shouting and screaming. We were on the verge of chaos.

I was taken to the front, to start singing with the people. But when I got to the microphone, it did not work. People started shouting and I tried without the microphone. Fortunately that went well, people quietened down again. I asked people to get up and start singing with me. The mood changed again to a euphoric one. These volatile changes of mood were quite frightening.

The church council has decided that we may stay until Friday.

Wednesday 11 October, 13.45 hours

Yesterday evening around 10 p.m. we got many visitors in our church corner and we sang. The church was quite full again and many people came up to us. We distributed song sheets and sang for one hour while the church was full and people stood in groups talking, or just sat or sang. Finally Mathias played the organ and then Boehme came from the SPD and gave a reasonably good speech. After that came an open discussion, which was reminiscent of parliamentary debates (only in our parliament we do not have any debates). Experts arrived who had been invited to our debates, which helped, and the whole event was a success. It is a new and vital hope for us, that broadly based discussions can develop. We have a new start and I hope we are not going to be pushed back; but our way is strewn with rocks and very long, and reading the newspapers today it is enough to make you shudder.

23.15 hours

Now it is quieter in our church than on previous days. I have just talked to Wolfram. It looks as if about ten people want to go on fasting and this will be possible in the Friedrichsfelde Church. We are going to move on Friday. Today there were demands for a continuation of meetings for our fasting group. I do not want that for myself.

Thursday 12 October, 21.00 hours

A discussion is in progress with eight representatives of the different opposition groups about the situation here. The debate is heated. Marianne has openly demanded the resignation of the Minister for Home Affairs and Security. I am still thinking about meeting two representatives of the local technical college for film-making. They want to make a documentary with me tomorrow. I am in the title role, describing the events during the last ten days.

Still, our struggle is not yet over. On the contrary, all is drawing to a climax. Many people are sending us their expressions of protest. An ever-growing section of the population is on our side, but many are still silent.

Friday 13 October, 00.30 hours

We have arrived in Friedrichsfelde. The church is small and peaceful. We are sleeping in the organ loft and there are only nine of us. We are all glad to be here. Yesterday, in Gethsemane Church, we experienced a difficult situation. Edith, who is in our fasting group, had been showing signs of stress. She seemed suddenly to have been overtaken by persecution mania. She took the microphone and said that all our organisations, even the Church, has been infiltrated by the Stasi. After that outburst I had to take the microphone and I said that we must not let ourselves be defeated by mistrust and that we are not afraid of Stasi presence, that we did not know what Edith had seen, but that those whom she had mentioned were innocent. Afterwards I talked to Edith. She, though, was absolutely convinced that she had acted correctly, but she thanked me for my presence and felt that the fasting had helped her. (The remarks about the Stasi were upsetting for the thousands of people listening.) Naturally there were Stasi present in the church. They had frequently approached me, sometimes pretending they wanted my autograph, sometimes to provoke a quarrel. One of them stood in front of me for days on and off, his brutal face staring at me. I only found out over the next few months that certain people within our closest circle belonged to the security forces [Stasi]. I could not believe it for a long time.

Saturday 14 October

Now we have arrived at the target date for the end of my fast. We are sitting in this beautiful old village church with a group of ten people and the same number of guests. We are in the vestry. There is a bench of lighted candles in front of a beautiful wooden cross. On the wall all the notes, letters and documents we received in Gethsemane Church are pinned up. It is cosy and pleasantly quiet here.

Early this morning Uwe and Kerstin came to start filming. A bit odd they should want a documentary film with me in it. How will my life progress from here?! I can't make plans yet. Will I be able to get a visa for the Soviet Union?

Gabi and Meikel are getting married today.

What will it be like when I start studying? It is possible that in such a framework I will find it easier to get permanent employment.

I would like to put my mind to thinking which opposition group I would most like to join.

Reflections

Meanwhile a year and a quarter have passed. In the centre of Leipzig where I am studying theology, vigils and protest demonstrations are taking place. The reason is the Gulf War. But very few young people take part. Many of those who were once active feel that they are either too busy or too tired now.

When I think back to autumn 1989 I remember 9 October and 4 November as the decisive days. On 4 November in Berlin's Alexanderplatz, we had the longest protest demonstration in the history of the DDR. At least 500,000 people from Berlin and the surrounding area had come to stage an impressive and creative event, demonstrating in favour of the renewal and change in the country, and not reunification. I believe that the sudden opening of the wall a few days later was a skilled manoeuvre by our old leaders to deflect the anger of the people from themselves and the real problems. Nobody outside the DDR can imagine the shock many DDR citizens experienced when they first visited the west. Compared with people in the west, they were nothing and they had nothing. The self-confidence they had gained during the demonstrations was soon lost. Scapegoats were soon found for all that had gone wrong before.

I am again in opposition to 'Democracy Now' and I am trying to keep my connections with our eastern neighbours. But our contacts are more fragile now we belong to the rich west with a hard convertible currency. Without having moved, I am suddenly living on the other side of the boundary between the First and Second Worlds. The day of unification was for me a day of sad farewells; not from the political system, but from the land I grew up in. I don't know if I shall find a home in this newly developing country. Discussions of whether there could have been an alternative to the present development are fruitless. But the experience of the power of protest without force during autumn 1989, with many different sorts of people all under one banner, will always be a sign of hope for me.

Leipzig 25 January 1991

Anke Höhne, aged 20, Potsdam
IT'S OVER!

It is over. The dream is at an end. I did not want to believe it. Now, just look – each day I see it in print, hear it on the news. Anke are you deaf or blind? Perhaps I do not want to believe it. The images of 7 October 1989 are deeply imprinted on me: the demonstration of 'counter-revolutionary elements', 'enemies of the state', and 'insurgents' (or agitators). Meeting the security service, the army, the police and the FDJ Ordnungsgruppen [Federal German Youth Organisations] ... was a traumatic experience for me. I asked myself if a number of them might not have preferred to be standing on our side.

During the confrontation with my contemporaries belonging to these organisations, I felt that we were a split generation. The split divides our society: the ones who have adapted themselves, those who sail with the prevailing wind will be on top in any system and those who do not easily agree with the status quo will remain uneasy and on the alert.

Out of the impotence of the first hot weeks in autumn 1989, the feeling that 'we are many. We are the people. Together we are strong', arose quickly.

However, that did not last long, the vent (or safety valve) of 'frontiers are open' on 9 November fulfilled its purpose. All of a sudden people had other things to do ... Who went on to the streets (just when that action would have been so significant)? We were easily satisfied and trusted the promises of the politicians. Still they continue to make their calculations without us, only now there are different politicians, who don't ask us about our opinions any more.

Have I done enough? I often ask myself that, and am not satisfied by the lack of an answer. I have also been quiet too often and for too long. It frightens me when I hear people talk (in the streets, in the cafés, at work or at school), saying that they had 'always' been against it and that they had always had their 'own opinions'. I have often wanted to ask them: 'Well then, what did you do?' 'You can't do anything about it' – I guessed that might be the answer, and it usually was. To admit to one's own shortcomings is probably the first step on the way to a conscientious and truthful life.

For a short time we felt as if we were the people, many people who had desires and hopes in common. Now everyone goes their own way again, many people sit in their homes, in their flats, in front of their television sets again. Once again events occur which concern us, upset us, but we're not in a hurry to rise again. Then our cup was full. Then – as if it had happened decades ago.

And now? Germany is one country again. But it is not my country. West Germany was and is alien to me. I was born and brought up here. It is odd that before the 'hot autumn' I often yearned to be far away and could not identify with this being my country. Then, after the fall of the wall and when reunification appeared to be a reality, only then did I start developing infantile feelings of love for my country. It was my country which was gradually being straightened out, where it was considered 'suspicious' to still be owning a DDR flag, let alone to fly one.

Now I live in 'Deutschland'; even to speak this word used to almost be a crime.

My family have always existed by adapting. They weren't satisfied with the situation in the DDR, but they lacked the courage to say so out loud. I never would or could fully understand that. To free oneself from a home where anxiety rules demands much self-confidence and decisiveness. Nevertheless, I distanced myself step by step. At an early age I went my own way; Church and friends helped me. Had my parents known about all my activities, they would certainly have stopped me. I know they were always concerned about me. However, it was precisely our fear which paralysed us for decades, and which we had to set aside in order to free ourselves. We also had to free ourselves from our feeling of cosy inactivity.

I am still on my way, and want to free myself from my chains. I know I shall never achieve that totally, but I shall at least try.

Katrin Klatt, Neuenkirchen/ Greisswald

THE OLD MEN

The old men still stand up whenever the National Anthem is played. Whose text they have forgotten.

The old men talk of the Third Reich, of the rebirth of Germany, of the first hours of the reconstruction. They break their speeches (for applause) for the other men.

Once the old men were workers. They later talk in the greatest detail about the working class. Today they are a class in themselves.

They babble through. Through our lives. The old men close the borders round their country, like the white shirts round their sick hearts. They sing solemnly and singly about the free German Youth.

The old men stand up again.

Peggy Einenkel, aged 16, Frankfurt am Oder

THE YEAR OF CHANGES

Hello. My name is Peggy Einenkel and I live in Frankfurt on the Oder. I'm sixteen years old and am coming to the end of the tenth year at school. Exams are looming.

A short while ago I was asked at school if I was interested in writing a story about my feelings and thoughts about the last two years, and sending it to Berlin to be included eventually in a book being published in England.

Cold and hunger have never been part of my life. My parents have always been able to give me a happy home life and I found security with my family and friends. I am healthy and if I was ever ill mum would look after me and we could always call on a doctor who would render his expert services free of charge. Both my parents work in vocational training. My sister is five years old and goes to nursery school. We live in a modern flat which has hot/cold running water and central heating and costs 100 DM/month in rent. We own a car and have a garden on the outskirts of town. I am a happy and contented person. I am saddened when I hear of children starving in the world, and nations fighting wars against each other – and even in some of the most fantastic cities which I have been allowed to learn about, people have to beg on the streets.

I am also afraid that the current insecurity of people in our country is spreading and could get worse. There is good and bad in every big change. Good and bad for everyone concerned. I am happy to be still young and to be living in these times which have such an important place in our country's history.

Exactly what was the cause of this peaceful revolution? I have thought for a long time about it. This revolution has brought change to absolutely every realm of life – school, work, leisure time and politics. Quite simply nothing has stayed the way it was. It is particularly difficult for us young people to think about it all, because we were born into these times and were taught only about the things that did not harm the socialist order in society. The people who brought us up had to influence us so that we would be turned on by their regime. The same was to be true at school later on – we were only able to develop thoughts between guidelines so that we didn't know and weren't taught anything different. And many people believed that everything had to be that way to secure a bright future. That is why it is terrible that some people reproach others who stand for goodness and had faith. I had this experience myself in my class at school, from a schoolgirl who used to be hypocritical about her school reports. She spoke just as you would have expected. Expression of personal opinion was only given guardedly. And these schoolgirls used to mock the rest of us because we believed in something good.

The revolution was necessary to break apart the wrongs of home policy. It had to change, because no trace of genuine socialism was left. But the people who impress me are those who stand up for the ideas they truly believe in, and who are to this day loyal to their ideals. I prefer them to those who change their mind for whatever happens to suit them best at the time.

I can still remember April 1989. I yearned for that day: the day when my classmates and I would join the ranks of the grown-ups. It meant nothing to us to vow to socialism, since we already believed that mankind's only future was in a socialist world. We didn't know of any alternative to that authoritarian socialism. We believed in the text of the vow 'Work hard and do everything possible for the good of the citizen.' Who would have thought that the people who had selected the text would be the last to uphold it.

Part of the ceremony was the presentati on of a book (to each of us) entitled *The Meaning of Our Lives*. It makes me angry whenever I reflect on this book: it contained the names of great people from different centuries, which were used to encourage the personality cult of Erich Honecker.

All German fairy stories begin with 'Once upon a time'. The fairy-tale we are currently experiencing begins: 'Would you have known three years ago that it would ever come to this?' I can recall a speech made by Honecker at the party conference – it would have been his last – 'And the wall will stand for another hundred years.'

I ask myself how the leader of a nation could be so wrong. He was well aware of the country's problems, because he had total supervision of the people. But he was not the only one who couldn't do his economic output sums properly.

The ministers in his charge were also to blame – they had reported exaggerated daily production figures. A joke about this went around the country. It revolved round the fact that a worker told his boss that only 60 per cent of target had been produced. The boss knew how different this figure should be; his job depended on it. So he fiddled the results and submitted higher figures in his report to his seniors. And so it went on – every chief added on a bit, right up to those in the ministry. The result of this was 115 per cent of the target, not 60 per cent. The consequence was higher bonuses all round. That's how the money was squandered. The upshot is today's state of bankruptcy.

That's the way it was in all areas. When it reached the top – everything was OK. If the message of the worker had been used constructively all this trouble could have been nipped in the bud.

The same was true of culture – the theatre, literature and other areas – it was under pressure. My grandmother explained to me that in Leipzig where she lived and worked she ran a large choir of male and female singers. She also ran an amateur dramatic society. But she gave these up one day, for the following reasons. All the songs she selected for the choir had to be submitted to the cadre leaders, who tested whether or not they were loyal to the state. They often demanded that the Red Flag come into the song somewhere. If that wasn't done the song was left out of the programme. Another time she organised a Christmas fairy-tale for the theatre group to perform for the children of the factory workers. In this fairy-tale ('Hansel and Gretel') angels appeared in the second act, to protect Hansel and Gretel in the forest. That was prohibited: she had to substitute elves for angels. At the end of the tale the entire cast had to sing a song: 'When emergency is at its peak, God the Father reaches out to us.' And Gran had to change that: she had to replace 'God the Father' with 'someone'. She produced the show, but resigned from her honorary post soon afterwards.

The church shared the same experience; preachers were put under the same pressure. True enough, the church wasn't banned, but priests could only give very restricted sermons. They were always on their guard.

When I learned all this, I began to consider where the border lies between right and wrong. My parents reinforced this – they taught me to make up my own mind and not to blindly believe everything that was put forward in the realm of politics in school.

Because supply was a problem in the DDR and the people had to go without fruit panic buying set in. If something became available, people would buy more than they could afford out of fear that tomorrow there would be nothing to buy. I saw this for myself when I worked two years ago during the school holidays as a salesgirl on the fruit stall in a market. That is when I first noticed the inequalities in the distribution of goods. I often had to tell shoppers that the goods they wanted had not been delivered, even though I knew this was not true. But so little arrived that it seldom got as far as the customers – it was often stashed behind the counter. It was the same for textiles and many other goods. Some counters near us only sold to the privileged few, such as government employees, who could not relate to the shortages experienced by common people. The privileged few had everything. Is it any wonder that discontent developed so quickly?

The same was also true of travel. I knew that kids who were in the Free German Youth movement could go to the so-called 'capitalist west'. Naturally there would be some sort of representation of the state security on these trips, and they would ensure that no one talked to foreigners.

Everywhere large numbers of people gathered secret police would be present, and it was the public awareness of this which made a revolution inevitable. Overseas it has become common knowledge how the state security operated. How can a state achieve greatness if it suppresses its people in such ways?

My grandmother once told me that several employees (mostly directors) were forced to visit colleagues during the weekend to check up on whether or not they were watching western broadcasts on television. If they caught people they had to dismantle the receiver and aerial. If a state is so afraid of the truth how can it last for ever?

The fact that so many people tried to cross the border illegally is a reflection on that. A cousin of mine went to a great deal of trouble to leave his homeland and family to go to Hungary and Yugoslavia. He wanted the freedom to make his own social decisions. At first we were very disturbed by his decision, but maybe these 'border hoppers' helped people finally to wake up and find the courage to break their boundaries. They didn't want to leave their home – they wanted to travel, discover new things and then return to their birthplace.

My uncle in Leipzig with whom I often discussed my feelings, told me that socialism was good but that people were not yet ready for it. How right he was! I think that people in their current development cannot build real socialism because the powers of materialism and the ego are still too important. One person wants to have more worldly goods than the next; the search for power and money increases drastically year by year. I often wonder how this will develop further, whether people will wake up and recognise their mistakes. It is the same with protection of the environment. It takes a lot of courage to commit oneself to peace and freedom. So much has still to be done for the Third World.

How many more children must go hungry? I take pleasure in the fact that so many artists are really putting themselves out to help the people of the Third World. A good example of this is the great piece, 'One World One Voice'. Art can play a great part in making people reflect on their situation – through plays, books and songs. When I leave school I hope to take up an artistic career.

Last year I had the great chance to go on a ten-day school trip to Spain. This was only possible because of the new era in which we live, which forbids nothing. Everyone can travel wherever they want. I got to know much that is beautiful and interesting in Spain. Above all – people. Because I had learned English for more than four years I could talk to the Spanish people and French tourists. I learned a lot about Spanish history on several trips to the countryside. The landscape was incredible. How wonderful it is to be able to travel like that – without borders. Before, we were totally screened from the rest of the world: now we can make up our own minds about other countries and life there. Now we can discover the truth. Before we were constantly under the influence of the government, which reflected things differently to how they really were. Now we can understand our neighbours.

The only countries we were allowed to visit were the USSR, Poland, Czechoslovakia, Hungary and Romania. I have been to Hungary three times with my parents. We have not been able to go for the last three years, since prices rose so much that one could only get by with Deutschmarks – which we did not have. Our 'Ostmark' was useless. The West German tourists could afford all the hotels, luxuries and of course shopping. My grandmother went to the USSR several times, and discovered that even in a socialist country like Russia there is a big difference between visitors from east and west. The tourists were put up in separate hotels. The food was different in the restaurants. They could buy good artefacts with their money, but we could only get inferior goods from special stalls.

On a return journey from Russia my grandmother and my parents had to stop over in Prague because the flight was grounded by fog. Again there was discrimination between east and west. East German passengers had to sit on their cases all night long in the departure hall, whereas the West Germans were put up in hotels. All of this has hurt our people. They have always been treated as second-class citizens. We former East Germans have it good since much has changed here, but there are eastern countries like Poland and Romania where people are still living as we did. Knowing this distresses me a lot. As the borders opened many, particularly youngsters, were crying 'Freedom'. What had they imagined it to be? Freedom is not just being able to travel abroad. Freedom is surely something more than that. What is lacking most of all is spiritual freedom, our own political opinion, free thought. How many young people have thought of that? Mostly they think only of material things.

I see a lot of things in my class. Some schoolchildren think that they are so free that they can be unruly towards the teachers. They are often shameless and arrogant. They think that the teacher can't take them to task over it. Yet we shouldn't forget that the teachers themselves were often in deep conflict with the material they had to teach. They often had to teach the children about things they knew were falsified in the textbooks. How hard that must have been for some teachers. They could do nothing about it. State security was so tight. Good teachers must have struggled to preach against their conscience. In my opinion these teachers have earned the respect of the schoolchildren. All too often when I confront classmates with this they laugh at me. Luckily it's only a few. Most share my view.

Crime has risen here; the word freedom is misunderstood. People who offend against other individuals or the state by robbing or vandalising public property are hurting themselves in the long run. Whatever they destroy has to be paid for by the state, which means that the state will not be able to do other things that are needed. In social areas like pensions or health care the money will be lacking. Everyone can contribute through good behaviour to our recovery. It is a shame that it is the anti-social elements, which every country has, who cannot or do not want to understand.

Now I would like to discuss the thing that has affected us most over the last two years. And this is it – how could 'the opening of the wall' be different? The level of emotion which ran through the people was indescribable. The people who were in Berlin on that day will never forget the feelings of inspiration.

They put their arms around one another, regardless of

whether they knew each other or not. Two of my uncles who were working in Berlin heard these events on the radio. They were already in bed. But they got up and got dressed, because they wanted to see it for themselves as they could not believe what was happening. They ran to the old wall and actually went across into the other Berlin. It was incredible for them and they ran with the others through the streets, with an amazing sense of joy. It was the greatest moment of their lives. Yes – to be suddenly free can only be appreciated by those who have been oppressed for decades.

Well, we have all got so used to the new way of life that it is almost taken for granted. Now we must hold on to our progress. We must take care not to dispose of the good with the bad. To do that would be a shame! We too had our social achievements, for example kindergartens, outpatient care, subsidies for food and shelter, and secure employment. Of course under the old regime a lot of jobs were artificially created which were unnecessary – including the thousands of Stasi employees who were only there to pry. We now see the consequences in the high numbers of unemployed in our country. Our people were hard-working, at least the majority. The former government should have this on their conscience too. It had run the economy badly and deceitfully. We have all had to suffer for it.

But we do not want to lose courage and we have to try to start again. Everyone has to help. We cannot simply *take* for ever; no, we have to make sacrifices.

I hope we succeed and that every citizen of our country shows the will to help us reach our goal. I mean to do as much as I can to contribute.

May it succeed!

CZECHOSLOVAKIA

The 'Prague Spring' of 1968 was crushed, its 'socialism with a human face' is said to have inspired Gorbachev who made friends with some of its prominent representatives in Moscow's Law School. In 1977 Charter 77 was formed: a circle of people monitoring abuses of power and human rights. Czechoslovakia was in the grip of neo-Stalinist leadership throughout the 70s and 80s. But in 1988, the commemoration of the twentieth anniversary of the invasion by the Warsaw Pact troops, and in January 1989 the commemoration of Jan Palach's death by self-immolation twenty years earlier sparked off a new wave of open protests. The police were out in strength in the streets. Something was in the air. 'There will be strikes,' I was told. Yet there was no sign of a change of heart by the hardliners. The 17th of November 1989 was to mark the death of a student killed by the Nazis in 1939. The student demonstration took a different turn. Orders came for the police to cordon off the students; severe beating and battle ensued. It is known that the police acted on government orders to destabilise the situation. Gorbachev's visit earlier that year had signalled to those in the government who wished for the Czechoslovak version of *perestroika*, that change to follow his policies was possible. The liberal Communist Party members' strategy backfired, though. They didn't gain the upper hand; on the contrary, they lost to the people. A general strike was declared in support of the students' initiative. 'We have had enough' and 'Down with the government; they have lied to us again!' were some of the slogans. A nationwide network of strike committees under the auspices of the Civic Forum sprang up. At the beginning of December the old government fell, and Vaclav Havel, the imprisoned Charter 77 activist, became President. He is much loved and admired for his moral politics, and his role is likened to that of the first Czechoslovak president in 1918, T. G. Masaryk. One should perhaps add that his 'progressive' government conspicuously lacks women. Now the Civic Forum has split and gone, the country is going through its own crisis of whether or not to purge the communists, and the old frustrations of privilege and hardship are back on the agenda.

Population: 15.6 million
Capital: Prague

1918 – Declaration of independence after the break-up of the Austro-Hungarian empire; T. G. Masaryk becomes the first president.
1939 – Invasion by Nazi Germany; declared a German Protectorate of Bohemia and Moravia, with Slovakia an independent Fascist state.
1945 – Liberated by the Red Army.
1946 – Coalition government; 38 per cent of votes go to the Communist Party in free elections.
1948 – A Communist coup to gain complete control; Gottwald as Prime Minister.
1952 – Biggest show trials followed by executions of Slan-

sky and others in Eastern Europe outside the Soviet Union.
1962 – A five-year economic plan abandoned; attempts at economic reform.
1968 – The 'Prague Spring' with A. Dubček as the new leader wanting to reform communism from within; August invasion by Soviet-led Warsaw Pact troops.
1969 – Jan Palach immolates himself in protest.
1970s and
80s – Period of 'normalisation' and neo-Stalinism under G. Husák.
1989 – The 'velvet' revolution; creation of the Civic Forum, a broadly based movement that assumes power; downfall of the Communist government; V. Havel as the new President.
1990 – First free elections, Civic Forum has a majority; start of denationalisation.
1991 – Split of the Civic Forum into two political factions/parties, its dissolution. Parliament agrees on the new name: Czech and Slovak Federative Republic.

Marek Šváb, aged 15, Praha
WE WANT ANSWERS!

The 17th of November 1989 was for me a completely normal day, and it was the same until around the 19th or 20th, when the TV started broadcasting that a demonstration in Prague had been suppressed. People were agitated and took to the streets. They demanded an explanation. It was given to them, but it was not exactly truthful. 'This demonstration is against the law!' People became more agitated and restless. They went out into the streets again, to find out the truth for themselves. From the famous balcony on Wenceslas Square the Prague population was informed of the consequences and details of the 'uprising'. It was no longer an uprising, it was a revolution. What was left then was the ČKD [Prague's largest heavy engineering factory] to boo off Štepán and that was that. Other factories joined ČKD and the government fell. This is what we call our 'velvet revolution'. The reality is not quite like that and I ask myself: where are the others like Husák, Jakeš and the rest? Why was only Štepán punished? And all in all, if Gorbachev wanted to take over Czechoslovakia, he could have done that, and finished. But that would have been the Third World War. This is why I feel angry that the other men who sent thousands of people to their death were not punished. Now they are peacefully enjoying their old age. Some of them have so much arrogance that they criticise today's state of things. I personally think that I'm not the only one who demands explanations. Don't ask me to believe in miracles.

Anonymous Woman Student, aged 18, Praha

LIES AND MORE LIES

I was not interested in politics until I was about fourteen, till I finished the basic grade school. All I knew were the main ideas of communism, and believed that one day we would truly arrive at a just communist society. It somehow escaped me that these ideas were very different from the reality.

Gradually, I began to be more curious about what was happening around me, and started to learn from different sources about the forbidden films, books, underground samizdat literature and the dissident movement. What I knew about the year 1968 were only fragmented and inaccurate pieces of information.

They taught us that the Charter 77 was a club of criminal elements who allowed themselves to be hired for the money of evil capitalists to undermine our republic. The capitalists were apparently worried that their people would want to demand some of our socialist achievements, would refuse to work for them, would come out on strikes and would want to take the revolutionary pathway of building socialism. That is why we have the Stb (the secret police), who are on the lookout for the undercover agents and who fight against terrorists.

I lived through 17 November and the events that followed in fear and tension. I was afraid of violence, but people surprisingly quickly 'changed their coats'. I tried to orient myself as fast as I could in the new situation and gain maximum information. Lots of things shocked me – in the positive and negative senses of the word.

I find contemporary political events (for that read 'pigs muscling for the troughs') deeply distasteful. We still don't have a free and independent television. I try to read as many of our dailies as possible but have the feeling that there are still many things that are unjustly concealed from the people. I wish that I was mistaken.

Lenka Bárczayová, aged 16, Ostrov
nad Ohří

GREAT BEGINNING AND THE HARD TIMES TO COME

My name is Lenka. I am sixteen years old and am in my third year at high school. I live in Ostrov, a medium-small town near Karlovy Vary on the border with Germany.

Since I was six, my family has been composed of only three people. My mum, my brother who is two years younger, and me. My parents divorced. I don't have any contact with my dad and so my only patient willow tree that listens is my mum. Ever since I was tiny, she drummed into me two very basic principles:

1. Never bring a gypsy home.
2. Never mix in politics, because politics is filth.

Our life and all our efforts have been aimed at creating at home a private world without pretence, a world of total honesty. Thank God, we have managed it quite well. That meant that I knew every detail of how my mother, her siblings and my granny trembled with fear under one blanket in our flat above the garrisons in August 1968.

'Children, there will be war,' our granny then said.

Many times I asked with a hint of accusation why they didn't stand up against IT that time. It's only since November 1989 that I have understood how difficult it is!!!

It all came like lightning from a clear sky. But no. That

sky was already full of the grey heaviness of injustice and cries for freedom.

From our mass media ever since 1988 we had heard about public disturbances by groups of hooligans and subversive elements on Wenceslas Square. When we watched these same elements on West German television, they were normal, decent people who stood there, holding hands, sang our National Anthem, 'Where is my Home', and resisted the water cannons of the forces of order, our guardians of socialism.

When we went to school on Monday morning, 20 November 1989, there hung in the air a peculiar, menacing tension. It was as if everyone was waiting for some impulse. That came (though I can't remember its precise form), and we immediately started collecting signatures for a petition against the brutal intervention on Národní Street. Inside me there was a mixture of very raw feelings that we must rapidly do something as well as a great fear. The fear seemed to predominate. I was terrified that *they* would hurt us. I wanted everything to be behind us. Really, I wasn't at all brave at first. I couldn't exactly imagine how they could do anything to me, but there was a sensation that they could do anything they liked. I don't have an exact definition of politics, but this reminded me of it, and politics as we know is filth.

There was chaos around, uncertainty, guesswork. I lost 6 kilos by the end of 1989. I didn't have time to study, I just sat in front of the TV and devoured information about the unfolding of the 'velvet revolution'. It was a beautiful time. All the people on the streets smiled at each other, cared for each other, slowly started crawling out of the shells of their previous total apathy. On every coat and jacket fluttered a tricolour; we openly and publicly talked of everything that not long ago could be said only at home, and even then caution was needed: walls have ears.

Then came Christmas. Presents were usually bought right on Christmas Eve. Mr Havel as President came with his wonderful New Year's speech. There was love and happiness everywhere.

But it was as if all this beauty had disappeared in the snowdrift deep in 1989 and there was little left for this year. At least that is how it appears to me. The wonderful, loving atmosphere, the teardrops of happiness, are gone. Perhaps this is the natural law of cooling off, but it's a pity.

And what next? What disturbs me most are the shrieks and the behaviour coming from Slovakia. But it's better if I don't expand on this. Slowly but surely, I respond to the problems of Slovakia with an allergic reaction, and I can already feel an outburst of rude words coming on.

Quite a number of things have changed. What is sensational is that my mum was able to stand as an independent candidate in the local elections. This is despite the fact that she strictly distanced herself from all political developments in the past. When I reminded her of her principle number two, she sharply rebuked me: 'It was something entirely different then!'

However, I have a different heavy burden on my conscience which bothers my thoughts in the darker moments. I worry about how from January we shall manage our already not too great financial situation. I think we shall overcome it but I am very anxious about our mum. She is on her own and she is already waging a protracted war with money. She herself is worried and this adds lines to her face, and silver hair.

It will be very hard for some time, but somewhere at the back, or most likely in front, there flickers a light of love and happiness. Now it depends only on us whether this light comes closer or is extinguished.

Tomáš Brzobohatý, aged 24, Mladá Boleslav

'THIS' IS WHAT WE CALL A REVOLUTION

I would like, right at the beginning, to let you know that what is in front of you is not a literary masterpiece drawing on the events of the autumn of the year 1989, nor is it a deep philosophical treatise about the causes and consequences of that November revolution. I have no right to present such thoughts as I am not the author of that revolution, merely a witness, the kind of witness that can be found in every historical situation. The history of mankind has countless witnesses like this and all of us take from the given event our own subjective impression that can have distinctive colours, sometimes may sound even a little false, but what can't be denied is the authenticity of individual perceptions.

It's of course questionable whether or not this authenticity can be transferred to others who were outside of the events. So, here I present some of my feelings and recollections from the revolution, hoping that they will fulfil their purpose, but having one or two doubts whether they will be of interest to anyone but myself.

I have given this piece a title: '"This" Is What We Call a Revolution'. Why? The reason is quite simple. Until November 1989 I, together with my contemporaries, felt as if I was outside history. It felt as if what we experienced in Czechoslovakia in the eighties and before in my childhood in the seventies was something unchangeable, fixed, something that would continue in a similar form throughout our lives. Words like war, revolution, governmental crisis, general strike, overthrow and so on belonged to a different, to us a distant, world with which we would never come into contact (that is in all probability), and that we would never understand the meaning behind these words.

I know it sounds naive, perhaps even a little foolish, but we really grew up in times of silences and deadness. Those were the times of silent and dead smiles, silent and dead actions, I am afraid even of silent and often dead wishes. There was indifference to what might come or could come. No wonder, because the only event in my life that history noticed was the year 1968 and the Soviet intervention. But in schools these events were never mentioned or they were presented as something normal, self-evident, and although initially we were surprised that on our way to school we didn't see Czechoslovak soldiers in the nearby garrisons but soldiers of foreign troops, eventually, habit being habit, we accepted it, just like posters along the same route inviting you to a theatre performance. At most, these soldiers were a source of laughter when they tried in vain to whistle at the local Czech girls. Sometimes we even felt a little sorry when from the expression on their faces you knew that they belonged to a different continent than Europe and were so far away from home. But we would never be sorry for the officers. (It's nice to write this in the past tense.) There was no cause for that. Their red faces – an unmistakable mark of a high-ranking officer in the Red Army (you can guess the rank and the number of years served according to the shade of the red) – revealed that they lived rather well in our country and that they certainly didn't suffer from a shortage of alcoholic beverages.

But to return to my original thoughts. I wanted to say that people of my age looked at our grandads' generation with astonishment once we realised that they had lived through two world wars, the years 1938 and 1948, and other political upheavals. I am afraid to express the thought that bugs me somewhere at the back of my mind, but I must admit that we even envied them a little. And us? We learned about wars, crisis and revolutions, and what brought them about. Under revolution we were constantly taught about the October revolution of 1917 in Russia, and nobody said or wanted to say that something similar might come even during our own lives. In a paradoxical way, we often heard about the threat of war, most often nuclear, but all the phrases were drowned in jargon, and at the end it looked like self-indulgent socialist folklore. My desire to experience a real historical event undoubtedly influenced the way I approached our own revolution; the desire to capture it as a historical canvas. It may be visible from the account that follows.

Perhaps it's appropriate that I should write something about myself by way of introduction. I shall be brief; stick to facts. Being an admirer of Karel Čapek, I like his idea that a person is never as mistaken as when he says something about himself. (But I do think about myself and am by nature an introvert.)

My name is Tomáš Brzobohatý, and at the time of the revolution I was just over twenty-two and a half years old. I was a first-year student at the School of Economics in Prague, and up until then my life had unfolded without any great extravagance. I had eight years of basic education, four years of high school, A levels, six months of unhappy studies of chemistry at the university, six months of working at one of Prague's research institutes, two years as a conscript in the army (which is the only event to which I ascribe some significance in my life, as it was something out of the ordinary), return from the army, a further year of work at the same institute, being accepted at the School of

Economics, a degree of disillusionment after starting there, and then simply one day we didn't go to the school and went on strike instead. Apart from these biographical details, I have some artistic interests, am of good health — which under socialism was always a good phrase to use at the end of a biography — had several years of membership in the pioneers and then the Socialist Youth organisation which entailed a membership card and presence at the 1st of May parades together with the socialist working class. My parents belonged to the working class; they were workers, which under the dictatorship of the proletariat determined one's position in every other sphere of life. The 1st of May was their celebration, the day of Labour, yet they rarely attended. The could not make it; usually because of the demands of work they didn't have time. This is perhaps the only irregularity in my biography, though not unique: that my parents though working in the category of jobs designated under socialism as working class, were not trained for these jobs and the change in their occupation didn't result from a desire to better themselves and achieve privileges. I could best describe their belonging to this class as a higher expression of personal freedom, which, according to Marxist philosophy, one reaches through the experience of necessity. But I don't want to dramatise. My father was an officer in the Czechoslovak army and the events of August 1968 prevented him from reaching further fame in that line of work. It seems that he didn't quite understand the brotherly help and internationalism of the fraternal Warsaw Pact armies and saw them as intervention by an outside aggressor. As a result he had to leave his job and was glad that the court tribunal only pronounced a conditional withdrawal of freedom. My mother, of course, followed and had to leave her office job for which under socialism she could never apply again. I and my brother, though interested in smaller tanks than those that crossed our borders, had a definite minus sign on our files. I have often heard that the local ideological secretary Omamik, whom I didn't know or see, once or twice in my life recommended (or to be precise withdrew his recommendation to) schools that might or might not be suitable for me. He also fulfilled the function of youth careers adviser, which I am convinced he did entirely on his own initiative and diligence, and for which he took no special extra financial reward – but who knows?

This, however, enabled me to have closer contact with my parents, since they didn't disappear to meetings or other activities of socialist invention. And they filled me with occasional pride, never expressed, in who they were and in their behaviour. My parents also enabled me, perhaps more than some of my contemporaries, to form my own opinion and not to believe everything that was preached at school. Under the socialist educational system this was a far greater advantage than to receive the free textbooks or other gifts of that system. One disadvantage, though, could have been my perpetual distrust, fostered from my childhood, that whatever is presented to you in its official form, say from the teacher, is not to be trusted. This shade of mistrust will probably stay with me for the rest of my days, and I may not be able to do anything about it. But at least there is no danger of falling for any ideology or religion.

Now I want to turn to my own recollections of the November revolution. But just before that I shall make a detour to three events immediately before the revolution.

The first relates to the summer of that year, 1989, and took place some time in July or August when even outside Prague there began a campaign, spreading like an avalanche, of signing a petition of 'A Few Sentences'. I was visiting an old friend of mine from conscription in East Bohemia. We understood each other perfectly as far as our opinions on politics were concerned. I was really pleased to find out that even in our civilian lives, which were so different, he hadn't changed and we could still talk about everything with enthusiasm. He was one of those eagerly collecting signatures for 'A Few Sentences', whilst I, quite frankly, was afraid to sign just before the start of my studies in case I might yet again complicate my life. We hotly debated the political situation in Czechoslovakia, going from pub to pub. I need not emphasise that our discussion began to deteriorate with our consumption of alcohol. At the end, as my friend could not get through my defences against the petition any more, he concluded with the unforgettable words: 'You constantly pick on something that is not quite right in it, but fundamentally, you are scared. Believe it or not, you will see that something will be happening here in six months' time. Everything is in flux. And you'll see that Havel will be President by the end of the year.'

I just waved my hand in a dismissive gesture then, but my friend was right. In the next three months we had our revolution and Havel became President one day before New Year's Eve. Later, when I read some speculations particularly from the Sládek's Republican quarters about how our revolution was merely a farce agreed upon in advance, I lovingly recalled my friend's prophetic words.

The second event is connected with a different friend, whom I got to know only during the crucial period of the upheavals, and it is not as good humoured as the first one despite the fact that it often brings a smile to my face now. Just before the start of my studies I went on a working trip to a paper mill near the Austrian border. The borders then looked a little different from now, and it manifested itself every morning when we took the work train, dressed in overalls, to be checked by the special unit of the border guards, the same age as us, demanding to know what we were up to in that region. We were not up to anything, because it was the university that sent us on this compulsory work experience. And it was there that I and a good friend of mine met another would-be first-year student. We liked his interesting opinions and thorough way of analysing everything; and we were all that little bit older than the rest. We bought a pamphlet about human rights once and discussed it together. Another time he tried to convince me that Havel was really a good and courageous person, but as a literary man he was not so good. I replied that when I heard his talk on Radio Free Europe, I enjoyed it very much. When we were asked by the local people about our views of the demonstration of 21 August, the date commemorating the 1968 invasion, we all agreed that it was best not to say much since it is known that in these border villages every second person is a secret policeman. Thus we debated all kinds of things at length and formed a fairly trusting and inseparable trio. When we returned to Prague we kept our friendship going, despite studying and living in different places. However, one day at the beginning of November 1989 our friend all of a sudden disappeared without explanation, and with no trace. We both looked for him and during the revolution wrote him several letters, thinking that something must have happened in his family. But there was silence. It was only after some considerable time that a classmate met him on the streets of Prague. He looked positively displeased that he could not avoid the meeting and to a question about what he was doing, he vaguely replied that he was in a rush and would she excuse him, he had no time. This made us think about this friend again and about everything we had talked about and experienced. Gradually we began to notice certain details and make certain connections. His behaviour started looking odd, until one of us dared to pronounce what we were afraid to say and to this day I find hard to believe: that our intimate friend was probably set up as a secret police agent.

I still feel slightly faint and all sorts of dark thoughts go through my mind, wishing that I would rather something had happened in his family, that he had fallen ill or that there had been some disaster for which he had to leave his studies. I feel frightened of these thoughts but there is nothing to substantiate them and I will have to come to terms with the fact that the intimate and strong friendship that grew so quickly was not after all a friendship but a well played act on his part and naivety on ours. Occasionally I even race after an idea that he could have been sincere about our friendship despite being an agent, but that is probably very far removed from the truth. So I think through what would have happened if he hadn't disappeared, if there had been no revolution – who knows? For once it was different and in our favour.

The third event related to the pre-revolutionary days is closely tied to the days running right up to the revolution itself. At that time public interest focused on the then first man in the country, Miloš Jakeš. A pity this interest was not quite what he might have liked. People of all social groups and ages were spreading a huge number of jokes with Jakeš as the hero. The best known were stories about his numerous grammatical mistakes and slips of the tongue, and in particular his appearance at a secret party gathering at Červený Hrádek. I began to feel a sort of revulsion to some of these, especially as the word 'jakeš' began to serve as a synonym for the most commonly used swear word. And though I used the swear word myself, maybe with lesser frequency, I could not help thinking that it's a sorry nation where the name of the head of the state is used with a visible degree of contempt. True enough, nothing was happening: the ruler who was taken for an unrivalled idiot in his state was ruling quite happily and dictated the tone of life for those who were enjoying themselves so much at his expense. That signalled that something really stinks in this kingdom of ours, the socialist republic of Czechoslovakia, and that it's about time this madhouse is turned upside down – or continuation of life in this kingdom will go beyond the bounds of human comprehension.

So change had arrived, a change called the velvet revolution. I personally favour the word revolt, because revolt it was, and instead of velvet I prefer what one of the actors, Miroslav Horníček, called 'hopeful'. It's because I don't believe that now or any time in the future can a certain historical event cure all ills, help solve all problems, and just because it has taken place, create happiness in the course of its happening and through its consequences. But what I am convinced of is that each such event has within itself this boundless power and hope – it's there, available. The question remains what one does with this power. That indeed is much more complicated and twisted.

One other reason why I don't think the word velvet suitable is that though I am happy that no blood was spilled, nevertheless, I realise that things could have been different. The word velvet rounds off and softens the general consequences of that revolution: the way it affected individual people and the overall course of their lives. I shall never forget one incident which took place about a month and a half after the revolution. I was standing at a tram stop on a small Prague square in front of one of the national ministries. There I witnessed a row, the vocabulary of which is too indecent to repeat here. The expressions belonged to the most depraved underworld, though the three gentlemen who'd just left the ministry certainly didn't look as if they belonged to that. They were dressed in immaculate fashionable suits and carried their office briefcases. One had his face covered in deep purple and the other two men also looked close to a heart attack. They were using the expressions to accuse each other of who ditched whom in front of their boss, who was or was not a 'useless Commie', who was or was not without any real skills, was or was not fighting for a clear slate, and indeed was or was not fighting just to keep their position. Simply, this was a sad scene, and I felt embarrassed to be witness to such an 'intimate' conversation. But especially I thought that if anyone approached these three specialists from the ministry at that moment and appealed to them with the velvet and gentleness, they would hardly succeed.

Let's return to the beginning of the revolution, and Friday 17 November. I knew for some time that on that day there was supposed to have been a students' demonstration, but I was not keen on the idea because I still took it to be some sort of officially declared 'would-be demonstration'. Fortunately I was persuaded to come and so took part in the first and the more successful part of the whole action, marching from Albertov to Vyšehrad. I was happy and shouted all those slogans that called for change, some of which were quite senseless. I watched the people around and felt a real happiness in merging with the majority. I don't belong to those people who can be quite spontaneous, and don't easily give my soul or body to mass action. This time was an exception despite the fact that I sensed that the whole thing would not end in a simple action that evening. This came over me as the dead silence while we were singing our National Anthem was broken by the shrill of whistles. It was clear where this noise was coming from and by the strength of the whistling it was clear that there were more than a few of them. But my pleasure was not spoilt and I felt free and relaxed. Where this carefree sense came from I don't know; I had just come from a heavy and boring day of lessons. But today I know that this sense of lightness exists in such situations, even among people of my type who don't feel it on other occasions.

I wanted to continue on the march, but I was persuaded by a friend to return to the university to attend a lecture.

This friend reminded me that I wanted to take an exam in the subject. To listen to a friend, particularly when it is a good friend, can't do any harm, because if we hadn't turned back I can imagine what would have happened on Národní Třída. This way, we sat through the lecture and then ran back to where we thought the march would be, but by then it was cordoned off and we could not join it. We only observed the relief on the faces of those who managed to break through the police cordon to get out. On my way to the march I managed to get involved in a row in a half-empty tram with two elderly people, a couple of communist persuasion. They held the opinion that all the young people who took part in the demonstration should be locked up. We tried to convince them otherwise, but without success. What we heard from them, and I heard later on other occasions, was an argument that I fail to understand. It's the argument of the type: 'How old are you? – you can't remember anything, so what do you want?' I am afraid that this view has not died with the death of socialism, and may be quite a strong and damaging argument in future situations when people struggle to defend their views, their conscience and perhaps even their material privileges.

But the lecture we went to was not uninteresting. It was an example of how life can be capricious. Our professor, roughly in his mid-fifties, was talking about the economic situation in Czechoslovakia before the Nazi occupation, as part of the course on economic history. Because it was 17 November, he allowed himself to recollect how on the very same day he had gone with his mother in Prague when he was young to the funeral of Jan Opletal (shot by the Nazis). There he saw the students' anti-Fascist movement, and the enraged Nazis charging them. This lecture took place about ten minutes from Národní Třída (where this time the Czech police charged the students). It was spoken in a quiet and informed voice, without any affectation; the way in which violence is often spoken about in history lessons.

Over the weekend I was at home in Mladá Boleslav, and I listened with great tension to Radio Free Europe, trying to catch any news about Prague. I was very agitated by the information about the death of one of the demonstrators and by the rather pathetic eyewitness account of the whole demonstration by one of our contemporary writers, Eva Kantůrková, who phoned Radio Free Europe. Her account was coloured by literary pathos about the peaceful behaviour of the demonstrators, and their equally young opponents in police uniforms with a nervous expression on their faces. She finished with an appeal to the then Prime Minister Adamec to investigate the whole thing because he alone of the whole governing elite commands some respect; the nation does not see him as a political dinosaur, like the rest of the communist leadership.

I rushed back to Prague on Sunday evening in hope that the university would come out on strike. I prepared for none of the lectures any more. That Sunday I took the bus not to the halls of residence as was my habit, but straight to Wenceslas Square. I listened to the gathered groups of people, to the numerous different opinions, to the accusations against the regime. One particular speech by a rather elegant forty-year-old gentleman stuck in my mind. It appeared that what he found most objectionable about Jakeš's regime was the inability to travel to the west. Another bizarre experience took place under the statue of St Wenceslas, one of the symbols of this revolution. In the middle of a small group of people was a young man, probably my age, who was one of those who took direct part in the demonstration on Národní Třída. Across the whole length of his face, I can't remember whether left or right, was a dreadful swelling from being hit by a truncheon. He was telling the crowd about what had happened on Národní

Třída, and described how he had got his injuries. People listened holding their breath, then pitied him, jointly swore at the brutal commando, and the regime, but soon the debate turned to Mr Jakeš again and his ridiculous public appearances. The debate took on a more jolly nature and I watched the beaten-up student, how with a hand covering his injuries he attempted a smile during the funniest of the Jakeš jokes. To this day, I think that it was only an attempt.

I don't just want to criticise the revolution. I gladly remember the moments during those days when I experienced the greatest happiness. I was so carefree, so content, simply felt the pleasure that comes to people only when they have a sense of anticipation, put all their hopes and desires into something, maybe are a bit afraid too, but at the end all is well. Then, I'm sure you will agree, you experience the greatest, most truthful joy.

It was Monday, 20 November, the first day of the famous revolution and the most decisive week. At four o'clock there was to be a demonstration on Wenceslas Square. We went with a group of friends from the university, which now was on strike. We hurried because we were late, and felt some fear about how many people would attend after the Friday massacre, about what the atmosphere would be. I shall never forget the feeling that overwhelmed me the moment I stepped on to the square from a side street in Jindřišská. Everything was overcome, all my fears gone, and my hopes surpassed; I had never before seen so many people together. Wenceslas Square was full to the brim. You could not see where the crowd started and where it ended. At the same time the whole square was one movement, gripped by total euphoria. That day I gave myself without reservation to the real crowd enthusiasm and shouting slogans. In following days I began to think more, but on this first day, all those who came surely had the right to act foolishly, aimlessly, without thinking; simply to take pleasure in the feeling that we had succeeded, that these were the first successes of our revolution, that there were 200,000 of us, 200,000 with the same idea – that it was impossible to continue like this in this country, and with this way of life. Later opinions began to diversify, but this initial and decisive step was made. A mass of people arrived together, a mass that could no longer be labelled as shipwrecked, reckless, deranged. You couldn't overlook it from any of the bureaucratic offices, from any of the official limousines or bunkers, from any of the positions that talk of the leading role in society, the class perspective. That was the creation of the base so that everyone realised that something really was happening, that it was no longer a game or a tragicomedy.

What followed was a way of designating some sort of direction, leadership, organised shape to this – what sounds like a discredited expression – people's movement. The more concrete ideas about what we should fight for or against formed in the later days, but the first day was without raising one's hand a kind of all-people's Prague referendum that the fight had begun; that this time we were dead serious.

Not everyone took it as seriously, though. One of the most interesting figures of modern Czechoslovak history must be Dr Husák, in those days still President of the republic, who was cursed during the demonstrations, but who at the time was entertaining the Foreign Minister of Costa Rica at the castle, where together they were contemplating enhancement of future relations between the two states. To contemplate enhancing his relationship with his own people probably didn't occur to him. He probably resolved this question for himself some twenty years earlier.

I am quite interested in his political personality, because he was the leading politician in our country during the entire time of my childhood and adolescence, and I often wonder whether he ever admitted in his mind that one day he would have to abdicate and that he would end up in a similar position to some of his predecessors – on the sidelines, being gradually but rapidly forgotten by the population. This forgetting is a rather unpleasant reminder of how senseless and empty were his life's political efforts, at least definitely those of the last twenty years. But before he had become totally forgotten, he had to preside over a humiliating event, congratulating the new incumbents of ministerial posts whom he had previously put behind bars, such as Jiří Dientsbier. Then followed his televised abdication speech, in which he uttered a sentence that I shall never forget and in which he evaluated the era of his rule: 'We have done things good, less good and even evil'! It would have been fascinating to know which of the things he placed in each category, but he would certainly not answer such a question. But because during his rule more and more things were done in the name of the third category, the November revolution had to come.

Now I would like to stop and look at what is for me a slightly embarrassing moment from our revolution, which surprised me but which is more understandable today. It was on Wednesday, the third day of the revolution, that I went home to Mladá Boleslav in the evening. I took with me some posters and leaflets and was curious to find out what was happening in my home town. I wondered what my parents would say who, for the reasons stated earlier, had no cause to love this socialist regime. I wanted to see how excited my father would be. During those last twenty years, day in day out, even at times when our TV put out popular programmes followed by the whole nation, he would try to tune in to one of the foreign radio stations broadcasting to Czechoslovakia. I arrived home and was ready to share my enthusiasm about the revolution, about the atmosphere in Wenceslas Square. But to no avail. My parents were full of doubts, expectations about how it would all end, and they told me not to think that everything would be solved by this. I am sure that many of their worries were connected to my being on strike; some of their scepticism, though, originated from their experience in 1968 when the intellectuals, students and artists had also been full of enthusiasm. And the result? Pity, but the little interest they showed in the development of the whole situation took me by surprise. Today I understand, but it is still difficult to put it down on paper. Hopefully, the defeat of the Communists helped something, perhaps people like my parents received some vindication, but human life is so short, human fate and human mistakes so hard to reverse, and the bad human qualities so difficult to destroy.

The demonstrations on Wenceslas Square and later on the Letenská Pláň in the next few days absorbed me in many varied impressions, but despite the overall happiness I sensed some danger. The crowd clapped all the speeches made from the platforms and chanted slogans, some of which were even contradictory. I also thought: how come the whole of Prague is so united, but what will happen tomorrow when the demonstrators disperse home, after winning (it was still not altogether clear), and what if there are arrests – will these people come the next day? Will I come the next day?

And how will it all look after the victory? The economy, education, social care? I really don't know how those who clapped and sloganised thought about their future; how many thought of words like unemployment, lower living standards, loss of security? It's curious how these future problems flashed through my mind at a time when someone in the crowd fell ill or worse, had a heart attack. I think one person died at Letná and the demonstration was interrupted by the hooting of ambulances. As if that sound of alarm coming from the ambulance over one human life, quite a concrete, real life, not any of the slogans thought out by the nameless crowd, as if that symbolised my fear and my hopes about what would happen next . . .

This man who was taken away by the ambulance, with his minor or more serious health problems – how will he face his fate when the revolution is over and when he may be back in good health? What was his life under socialism like, how afraid was he or wasn't he, how straight or not did he walk, and why did he come to this demonstration? To show his face to his neighbourhood, whilst wishing to live the way he has always lived? All this, however strange right then, was going through my mind.

At one moment, I think, others came to a similar realisation when at the end of one of the demonstrations at Letná Miloš Zeman from the Institute of Prognostics said a few unpopular words. He read to this overjoyed crowd a few statistical facts about the position of Czechoslovakia vis-à-vis Europe and the world, giving the appalling life expectancy data. People shouted and whistled, blamed the members of the Politbureau, but I guess that at that time most of them knew that what was to come would not just be the changing of street names, building monuments to T. G. Masaryk, pulling down barbed wire at the borders, mass demonstrations, the giving out of honours to those who suffered, and general complaints about what socialism did to you, how dreadful it was and how much one needed to resist. Yes, Zeman reminded people with his plain facts that there might be something quite different to come.

I have lived through the general strike of 27 November: that was the main leading force of all the arguments on both Wenceslas Square and in front of our college. The strike was crucial – without it much could have been reversed – but at the same time it was a farce reminding me of the 1st of May celebrations. The only thing missing was the official platform with selected guests, but even that could have been found. What I remember is the long queue to the underground about ten minutes before the strike should have ended when the underground itself was to start again. I looked forward to this strike, thinking that I would live through something that I would always remember. But as with most events you dream of, the reality often stinks of embarrassment. A similar thing happened about a month and a half later when I looked forward to the moment when Václav Havel was being elected President. But what there was, was an unbelievable uniformity and herd-like behaviour. The way he was elected was unanimous and yet among those who voted for him were some for whom he had been the arch-enemy for twenty years. He and his way of thinking represented a threat to their way of life. They must have known as they were voting that it was precisely their kind who had lost their role in parliament at that very moment. It was a sad picture of those so-called representatives, and another insight into human fate. A pity that lots of them took part in some of the cheapest and saddest farces played in our country and nation.

I have some recollections of Václav Havel, too. When I saw his photograph for the first time I took him for a typical Prague inhabitant, someone who knows it all, and who is unnecessarily big-headed. But later he convinced me of the opposite. What a remarkable difference between someone's exterior and their soul. Another memory is of the post-revolutionary period. I don't know how many people in the world would queue for six hours in front of a bookshop for a book. Well, I was one of them, as were other Czechs. We stood that amount of time in a queue for the first edition of Havel's *Distant Conversations*, a book that didn't disappoint me and from which I often read, particularly the final passages, even now. I stood then in that queue with a friend who was a great fan of Havel. Today he shouts at the Republican Party gatherings: 'Enough of Havel, long live Sládek!', and when I reminded him of the bookshop queue he retorted that he never read the book and that he was not interested in Havel's gobbledegook. I think, and have told him so, that if he read at least the final part he might not be so keen on Sladek's demonstrations. But otherwise I am sad, though I am used to changes in people's perceptions, and feel that it's not the symbols but the people who are at the root of the problem.

Every time people discuss what the state security did during the revolution, I recall two incidents. I may be mistaken about the first one. It took place the very first day of the strike in a café near our college. Three of us students met there, probably to have a Coca-Cola, and we sat at a table and debated. There was a bloke sitting at the same table who was drinking his coffee remarkably slowly. His general expression was of someone fed up, laid back, yet he also seemed interested in our talk, though he didn't take part – unlike some café clever clogs. Though it was the first day of the strike, and we were full of new impressions, I tried to steer the debate away from the main topic. We started talking about Paul McCartney, sounding as if we were dead keen. My friends, without a word, accepted the change of topic and got involved. We later agreed that none of us quite liked our neighbour, and we were happy to having silently agreed.

The second incident took place a day later, during the time full of confusion about what would happen next. It was in Wenceslas Square itself, where near the statue of St Wenceslas a permanent gathering of people were endlessly discussing and solving the problems of the day, as well as waiting for the most recent information, confirmed and unconfirmed. One of the pieces of news that day was that the troops of the People's Militia were approaching and closing on to Prague. This information had its strongest impact just before lunchtime, when it was reinforced by further morbid news that a whole division and tanks were moving towards the centre of Prague. There was instant chaos bordering on desperation. It was announced that everyone should leave Wenceslas Square, particularly the top part. People started to go, but I and a friend didn't want to leave, though we were a little scared, because we were too curious as to what might happen. We took ourselves to the steps of the National Museum at the head of the square, which at the time of the revolution was a sort of watchtower. There were lots of people there, all discussing the latest dreadful news. Throughout our talk with other people I yet again noticed a man who watched us and who looked so nondescript, so totally faceless, and so much like our neighbour from yesterday, that I waited to see if he was going to take part in any of the debate. He didn't disappoint me and got involved in a truly original manner. He abruptly interrupted and said that a minute ago he saw tanks in Žižkov [on the outskirts of Prague], and that they would be here in ten minutes. Though we doubted his information, my friend and I went towards our college to find out what was happening. I can't remember what was going on at the college, but what I do know is that there were no tanks at Žižkov. So ... but who knows ... Maybe that man just wanted to attract people's attention. But I doubt it, somehow.

Among the most interesting of my experiences is something quite different, relating to one of the key roles of the student body during the revolution, that is their agitational role – though the expression is repulsive to me. During those days many of the students travelled and visited different factories, urging the workers to take part in the general strike. I must admit that this was quite interesting, not least because in my imagination it is what revolutions are supposed to be about. I went with another good friend. We met at our university and from its headquarters picked up a whole pile of leaflets and a list of enterprises that we should visit. We were also advised to get together with some artists (who were also in the forefront of the action) to avoid being seen as just foolish youth. We arrived at Mánes, the headquarters of the artists, and were not let down. Without much persuasion, we were accompanied by two people: a thirty-five-year-old pleasant, and probably quite well-known, woman sculptor and a bearded introverted graphic designer, perhaps ten years older than her.

I am not sure what agitational impression the three of us and the sculptor gave, but the graphic designer certainly didn't radiate much passion. He remained silent most of the day, or uttered a complaint that he had missed his usual morning coffee and therefore wouldn't be much use. Nevertheless, he supplied our expedition with a sort of wisdom and deliberation. To add to that, he unwittingly provided some entertainment when on our way to the first factory he asked what we students intended to do with them. The 'them' was meant to refer to the Communists, and it became clear that he himself was a member of the Communist Party. It transpired that he was genuinely frightened of our movement, which indirectly gave me a little confidence, maybe false confidence, and convinced me of the rightness of our action. Later, in another factory, when asked why it was important to have the general strike and to see the departure of Jakeš and the like, he came out with the argument that at a recent exhibition devoted to the Czechoslovak–Soviet friendship, they wouldn't let him put up a sign bearing Mikhail Gorbachev's pronouncement about *perestroika*. It was a strange sort of argument, especially taken against our points about the state of living standards, environmental destruction, freedom of the individual, etc. However, this scene was typical of what was happening in Czechoslovakia at that time. It was the first time in forty years that everything that was being said in the Kremlin and was holy writ in Czechoslovakia, all of a sudden was being censored, and with it the words of the Kremlin's leader. A new set of slogans began to appear. No longer 'The Soviet Union for ever and ever' but 'Romania for ever and not any other way.'

At the first factory we went to, we announced ourselves and were sent at once to see the director. He greeted us all right, but in every other respect he was unwavering. Though he admitted that the party leadership was not the wisest in the recent past, that some sort of change might be beneficial – what, he didn't elaborate – nevertheless, despite long discussion, he refused to let his factory take part in the general strike. His argument was loss of productivity, which would mean for him and the employees who supported him, the loss of bonuses and the 'thirteenth' salary (the one that comes after the end of the calendar year). That unlucky salary number was his sole argument which we could not bridge. We thanked him in a disappointed mood, exchanged smiles (whose was more honest or dishonest is hard to say) and left him, probably glad to get rid of us. We were leaving in a disheartened way when two workers stopped us. Before we knew what was happening, they had taken us to their work room, introduced themselves as representatives of the strike committee that had been set up only the day before, and expressed their surprise that we had gone to the director and not to them: 'Nobody listens to him here any more.' In the same breath, they told us that the factory had unanimously voted, apart from the director and the chairman of the old trade union, to take part in the general strike for the agreed two hours of total stoppage. Our mood returned to our fully blown enthusiasm and desire to continue to agitate. Delighted, we crossed off one enterprise from our list and set off to conquer others. We didn't give much thought to the fact that in reality we hadn't needed to do much agitation in this factory, and that we could have saved our time by asking for the right place and the right people.

A more interesting situation arose in a different factory. We didn't succeed, and were glad to get out of there, though I think that eventually they went on strike too. This happened on Wednesday, when it still wasn't very clear who would play the leading role in this revolution, and who would have the last laugh. It was obvious that what mattered in this factory was to know who the victors would be. We hadn't even passed the porter's lodge when a man, relatively young for a porter, stopped us, and I immediately realised that he was not the regular porter but an active representative of that famous and proud People's Militia. He didn't let us go any further. But even before that he made an impression on me similar to that I gained from my previous encounters with members of the secret police. He was colourless, weary, considerably uncertain of himself, but tried to cover this by pronouncing a sharp, quick verdict on us. But we didn't give up. After a prolonged telephone call, presumably to a high-ranking party official, the official appeared and at once expressed his negative attitude to the strike and refused to listen to anything else. He overlooked our two co-agitators and despite looking lustily at our female companion's see-through T-shirt, he wasn't persuaded. In fact he called in reinforcements, including another woman, for me a typical representative of the party secretarial corps of our socialist proletariat: a woman around forty, big, resolute, with forceful gestures and a forceful look in her eyes. She looked us over and assured us that our visit was of no use because a while ago the factory had been visited by a famous actor, whose name and title she pronounced in such a way as to emphasise the difference between him and us. Despite his popularity, he hadn't succeeded either. He was a sufficient example of the present agitation, and they had had enough.

Then a second reinforcement, a worker of about fifty, came along and asked the ever-present question: 'How old are you?' I admitted to my twenty-two years, at which point there was silence. He looked as if he was thinking something over, and then fired: 'Get out of here! You can't remember anything!' This was it, the generational argument again. This time, however, it touched me in a bitter sort of way and I couldn't control myself. I nearly hit the man, and there was almost a fight between me and the worker. Fortunately my friends calmed me down and I left the factory with a mixed sense of disappointment and failure. But it was only Wednesday, and a lot more things were to happen.

An even more bizarre impression came from our reception in one of Prague's large, well-known electro-engineering enterprises. We were admitted to the office of the party boss there, together with the chief of the enterprise People's Militia. We were investigating whether the People's Militia would come out against us if they received instructions from above. The whole conversation and atmosphere was rather poetical – we sat in deep swivel chairs and the room was dominated by a large portrait of Miloš Jakeš. Up to then I'd been used to portraits of the President, Gustav Husák, and now I was watching a picture of someone else. It had a strange effect on me. The whole discussion, which was not altogether stupid, appeared to be taking place, just like the portrait of a man nobody believes any more, somewhere in a vacuum. I had a distinct impression that what we were talking about, them and us, had no real value, that after a few days everything would be different anyway. I don't know where that feeling came from, but events later confirmed it. Though the party boss was then still sure of his position and his views, several days later he lost this certainty. The leading role of the party was removed from the constitution. The party bosses at enterprises had had their day, and the same was true of the People's Militia. We never received an answer to our question about the Militia's intervention. But the debate was a sort of checking each other out. They, and even we, were testing what the students' movement was capable of, how far we would go in our demands. We were aware of that, and tried to give an impression of a well organised student body.

So much for my observations during those turbulent days. The whole development certainly didn't disappoint my expectations, though I could not predict, and nobody could, some of the problems such as the Czech–Moravian–Slovak relationships, the growing criminality, the new intrigues within different political parties, and above all the fact that though people shed one totality, some seemed to long for another.

Two sad memories come to mind. One is linked to 17 May 1990 – the day of one of the most embarrassing of celebrations that I ever heard of. It was the six-month commemoration of the events on Národní Třída. I have no idea why, but people without being prompted began to kneel on the street, raised their arms towards the heavens and began to shout that they had bare hands. I didn't understand their actions. No one was taking their bare hands away from them. It was another bizarre picture by an unknown medieval painter.

Another sad impression was the call from a group of students about a stolen revolution. That is more understandable, yet it relates to the idea that the whole revolution was no more than a played-out farce, and that everything was manipulated from start to finish. For myself, I can say that during those November days, everything I did was my own decision, I had full awareness and full responsibility for my actions.

And my feelings now?

My wish to live through great historical changes has come

true. This helps me to see in a much sharper way, to take in all the things around me, and gives me a better understanding of myself. I see my life much more through the eyes of others. The days of the revolution remind me of a visit to a museum of people's best behaviour. Everyone was so kind to each other. My friends remark that they have never seen me so optimistic and full of joy as on the day of the demonstration at Albertov. The revolution did mark my life and my future. I can stop worrying about having a file kept on me somewhere, having to be careful what I say.

And I also think about what sort of a nation we are. Is democracy a universal medicine? Where are its boundaries? Who is the least dangerous politician? What of criminality? And where is the surrounding world going? Did all this have to happen? Which, in the light of the recent Soviet developments is a topical question? Was communist teaching bad in itself, in its core, or did it become evil because it was applied by a group of people with lesser morality? Was it all a utopia? What can we believe in? There are myriad questions. All I know is that the best attribute of freedom is one's own responsibility for oneself; that goodness is often the least visible of human characteristics; that truth can't be transmitted only as spoken information; that people should not have exaggerated illusions about anyone, but should not dismiss anyone too quickly either; that we too are responsible for those who rule us and make decisions about public matters, etc., etc. I try to understand some of these things. And I believe in mirrors. I think that every person, every society, every social order needs its mirror in which to see itself and its surroundings, in which to compare, learn, confront, gradually sweep away the dirt, improve and embellish. Of course, the first condition of any success in seeing oneself in the mirror is to look straight, without prejudice, with clear conscience and not with a constructed image beforehand of what one wants to see, or worse – how one wants to be seen. The fact that our previous regime was mortally terrified of such a mirror is without any doubt. Instead it erected barbed-wire fences, built walls, introduced censorship, and other similar novelties.

I have few doubts now too. For building up the foundations of democracy one needs some self-reflection but also enough democrats with skill. Where are they? I am afraid. I am afraid of myself; of my own inadequacies, of not being able to respond appropriately to future events, of not seeing who means well and who less well. I don't have illusions or too much optimism. I am merely curious about what will come and how I shall hold my ground.

Jana Kovačová, aged 16, Roudnice

BEFORE, THEN AND NOW

The days unfolded one by one in such a way that one didn't even realise it. As a child, I never thought that things around me could be different; that the empty phrases of the old, shaky men whom we were supposed to respect would go away; that in our free time we could do things that we enjoyed doing and not those that we had to do or that others did; that from the age of ten we wouldn't have to learn by rote and memorise the slogans of the Communist Party. Up to now, everything was so natural, at least for us.

Today, when I look back, I see how limited it all was. My life before was like a closed pot with its lid lifted from time to time. That was in the form of letters from friends, *émigrés* in America. Yes, I always knew that 'somewhere' there were people who had a better life, didn't have to queue for goods of low quality, and didn't have to face empty shelves. I created my own inner carefree world where . . . when I grow up I shall have all those things that they have over there. Everything will be free, people will be nice to each other, they will work with honesty, they will never face shortages . . . It will be enough just to do my schoolwork properly and be honest. We shall get to that point. I called that future, as it was presented to me so many times, communism. I believed in it.

The other rules and definitions from our compulsory lessons of civic education have long been forgotten. I only remember how the whole class trembled before each lesson because the words and slogans of our working-class people and the items in the programme of our Communist Party were all mixed up and we couldn't find any meaning in them. After a few of the unlucky ones were called out to answer senseless questions and then went back to their desks exhausted, the class began to get bored. We were equally disgusted with our history lessons. My enthusiasm for the subject dropped when after exciting uprisings or the discovery of the New World, we were fed the dates of the foundation of communist parties in different parts of the world.

I followed the TV only sporadically. The speakers never changed very much and what they had to say remained largely the same too. But when high-ranking personalities gave out prizes to the best pioneers in the country, I often wished that I too would be one of the best. Once, I confided this to my father. I interpreted his sigh and grimace as misunderstanding. So I told him my feelings in more colourful terms. When again I heard no words of support, I asked him why. To no avail.

Another event that sticks in my memory is my unsuccessful preparation for an all-out pioneer gathering. I carefully tied my pioneer red scarf so that both ends formed a perfect symmetry. When I was looking into the mirror, eyeing my costume of which I was proud and hoping that it suited me, my father came in. His outburst of disapproval and disgust was totally incomprehensible to me. Particularly, I was not clear why I should not have been dressed in that 'nonsense'. He forbade me to go. There are other ways to waste time, apparently. I didn't understand it, I only felt petrified about how I would explain at school the next day that my father wouldn't let me go. His words affected me deeply, they shattered the world in which I lived. I then learned why that 'circus' was a waste of time, including what was wrong with our president. I remember everything very clearly. But I understood only some of it, such as that our president is unintelligent, does nothing for our country, is manipulated by others who are as bad as him, he is a sorry figure. Also that my pioneer organisation means nothing, my civic lessons are full of untruths, etc. I did feel that in my life then there were certain conflicts, that something was not quite right. But I didn't really want to know why, because then I would have to admit that either they lied to us at school or that my father was wrong. Both of these were equally horrendous, unacceptable, unthinkable. I had to accept this deep rift. Surprisingly, I never thought that anything could ever be done about it. I felt a subconscious fear. But mainly, I was forbidden to say anything to anyone outside, including at school.

These years were so sleepy, as if we didn't possess any life of active fantasy. It was not lack of imagination or laziness. It was not aversion to work, aversion to thought. It was something entirely different. We were growing up under the ever-present cloud of fear, ever-present subconscious anxiety of school, of tests, of the teachers, of thinking that we might do something wrong, anxiety about not having enough money ... We could not openly talk about that, we didn't even know it. It was inside. Our initiative was inconspicuously eroded, brushed away. You felt that something in your life was missing, but you didn't know what and why. Even the fear of deviating from a given goal was depressing. Hold on, as they said, and you will be all right; perhaps you will be all right ... You are different, your style, your thinking is just off the mark, society will reject you and no one, not even a dog, will bark to remember you. From fear, of course.

This is about the future that awaited us, but luckily it didn't come to that. The fact remains, though, that the whole nation was accustomed to the fact that when problems occur *someone* would solve them: everything will be decided *somewhere* at the top. You just need to believe,

believe that what they do is right. In this passive world, I simply could not contemplate that life could be improved, that one could start even with little things, small things.

I come from Roudnice, which lies about 50 kilometres from Prague. Hundreds of people from this medium-sized town commute to Prague every day. Transport between the two towns is quite frequent. This is perhaps one of the reasons why news from Prague to Roudnice travels fast. On the evening of 18 November 1989, we had a visit from an acquaintance – a doctor. I only spotted his terrified face and then was sent to bed. The next day I heard about everything – no one could stay quiet about these things. By that time it was an afternoon, and my parents knew a lot more. They told me what had happened in Prague, what Mr P. had told them, who had the news from a direct participant in that bloody clash, including the later events. The die was cast.

The information was first confused, incomplete, conflicting. But something was definitely happening. It was like a gush of fresh air, an oxygen current. In the following days events took a much faster turn. The streets were full of various flying posters. Not many people knew what was actually taking place, what they were supposed to think about it. There was a spark of hope for a different future, different from what had been outlined for us. The spark grew into a flame and later into a bonfire. My parents went to Prague to find out more because the uncertainty about what was really happening and what could still happen was unbearable. They came back with a whole pile of posters, news and newspapers. One could not absorb it all, let alone understand it. But what there was now was an unshakeable, totally new certainty that *we* had the truth, and not *them*! Every day brought new events. We suppressed our fears (those that accompanied us our whole life) and trusted that if we joined together, if we 'fought', everything would end well. There was no other option.

At home we had daily debates, explanations, discussion of the individual news. Before me opened up an unknown world – of political events, of political connections. I felt an awakened sense of patriotism. I was hungry for every word, I longed for the truth. The truth that is real, truth without the wrapping of sweet words and promises. It was hard but beautiful.

In the evenings when we watched TV, I was often on the brink of tears. Many of the newscasters had shaky hands, their slips of the tongue multiplied. After a few days they were replaced by other newscasters, but even these were not quite sure of what to do with the news. Outwardly there were no changes, nothing was said officially. But the nation knew that now there was a big chance, a chance that it must not let go of.

Then followed really wonderful days. Slowly, every evening, crowds of people gathered in the town square. They all wanted to know what was happening. Those who were more informed read out messages or the new independent press. Initially the speakers stood on a simple wooden box and the light came from candles or torches. After a while the situation improved and they had a microphone, a little platform and speakers. This makeshift arrangement brought us closer together. People of the old type of thinking or staunch communists stopped attending.

At the end of November I saw for the first time the video recording of the events of 17 November. I started shaking uncontrollably and for the first time during those days I was gripped by terror. Real terror of other people's power, of the army, about our powerlessness.

The whole situation affected our everyday life. We stopped addressing our teachers as 'comrade' and began to call them the more respectful 'professor'. On our information boards we put up real topical news items, and changed them often to keep them up to date with new information.

The regular annual communist celebrations and the festivals of the Great Red Brother slipped into oblivion. But on the other hand, much information circulated about our very first president, T. G. Masaryk. More news from Prague arrived at our school every morning.

We wore the tricolour on our coat lapels, as if it was a sort of precious symbol. Often we told off classmates for their fear and cowardice when before certain lessons they took off their tricolours so as not to get a bad name with some of the professors. Sometimes we took courage and asked our teachers about their opinion on the political situation, simply, which side they were on. That was previously unheard of. Usually they cautiously moved the conversation on to other topics. I don't remember quarrelling with anyone during that whole time. Outside of political discussions, of course. Despite some people who stopped greeting us when they met my family, those with whom we kept in touch were exceptionally considerate, genuinely nice and attentive. One of the most beautiful moments was undoubtedly the keeping of the light vigil in front of statues of famous Czech personalities. In our town, for example, we have a statue of Jan Hus. After each meeting we would sing the National Anthem as a sign of unity. I began to understand its words properly and to feel them. People would hold candles in their frozen hands, their coats stained from dripping wax, it was so cold and frosty, but we all kept a smile on our face, our hearts full of expectation, hopes, certainties as well as uncertainties . . . In those moments we were so beautifully close to each other, one people who know what they want; one wonderful nation that has finally shed its burden and knows what it needs, what it's going to fight for. There was a strange, pleasant sense of intoxication, warmth that rose through the body. It was a kind of drunkenness, I wanted to cry and laugh at the same time. My friends' eyes and cheeks burned with excitement, our hearts overflowed with joy, strength ... After the anthem, we would lay the candles at the foot of the statue. Everyone was ready to offer help, advice. I took in so much energy then. I know for sure that I shall never forget those real days.

But a couple of years have passed and much has changed, much remained the same. Most people forgot the kindness and courtesy with which they behaved. They returned to the old tricks – fighting for their own position.

Long before the year 1989 my love of books led me to read some that were forbidden or were marked as unsuitable. I don't know who thought they were unsuitable, but it must surely have been a servant of the old regime. Lots of these books, instead of elevating the virtues of workers and peasant heroes or the stupidity of the bourgeoisie under rotten capitalism, told of the magic of the natural world, of genuine friendships, of adventures in the woods ... These were not samizdat literature, they were often tens of years old, stuck away somewhere in the attic. But they were worshipped with the same love with which they were written. Lots of such stories were written by Jaroslav Fogler, who answered many of the desires and needs of young people. Now, I felt, he could finally be appreciated. But ... as yet we don't know how to live in freedom. As soon as our chains from the past have been removed, we go for extremes. We simply don't know how to treat freedom. One of the surprising things is excessive praise of Fogler, or the elevation of the Scout movement into an ideal. They are good ideas, but many people don't know what to do with them. Scouts, for example, have almost replaced the old pioneer organisation. I feel shattered.

I think that our hopes, struggles and gradual disappointments have left their mark. We, as a generation, had to grow up very quickly. Out of the blue, we had to face up to new responsibilities for ourselves and face new fears of the not so rosy future. Lots of young people who see that what they have aspired to and in which they have invested so much of their energy is so distant, and that promises are not being fulfilled, have stopped believing in ideals. We all know that we have to make our own decisions about what we want to do, and that we will have to work hard, otherwise ... It's too sudden a change. From our early years, we had been used to everything being straightforward. Now we have to rely on ourselves. There are many new problems ahead of us. There is nobody to tell us how to solve them. We just need to believe in our own strength.

Petr Tůma, aged 24, Uherský Brod
FREEDOM AT A PRICE

Don't you think I should introduce myself first? It's good manners, I know. In that case – my name is Petr Tůma and I study medicine at the Charles University in Prague. So I am no Martian, but an ordinary citizen like thousands of others; with a body, arms, legs and a head. Yes, in particular the head, which has been here for the past twenty-four years, looking around, utilising those few per cent of its brain capacity which it possesses and which likes to doubt the world, and often can't stop wondering. The head is not saintly and does not believe in God. It is a hard and vain male knob, not much different from those others who first saw the light of day in Moravian Silesia. Despite my inborn modesty I have to state that Moravia is the most beautiful corner of the earth, and as a born democrat I shall forbid anyone to doubt that. So, that's that.

Before I came to Prague I lived my childhood and jumped through puberty in Moravia. Because I have fantastic parents and good friends, all those events passed without causing great bumps and I could file this chapter of my life into the category, 'peaceful, happy'. The fact is that unless I was at school, I damaged my hormones by playing basketball and athletics, or I used to play around on the guitar. Not that I was much good; perhaps I was worse than Dylan, because I would not have been able to earn even enough for salt water. I have learned how to kiss, and otherwise I have suffered through having my tonsils out and from private Beatlemania. And politics? I can safely say that it played an insignificant role. The year 1968 was taboo. For me it had no meaning. It was only through an accident that I heard about my father's leaving the Communist Party in protest. He never boasted about it. I don't think that my folks understood those events all that much then. They must have felt taken aback by it all. My mother, when she heard that there were Soviet tanks on our nation's soil, ran to the nursery school to pick me up and take me home. They have obviously been marked by the whole thing, but took it as their private affair and never wanted to burden me with it.

Only after I went to university and Gorbachev came – then Poland, Hungary and East Germany – did you begin to sense that something hung in the air. All in all it was clear that Czechoslovakia would not escape either. But nobody knew when.

I was not in Prague on the eve of 17 November 1989. I went to a friend to do some horse-riding and when I was hitchhiking back to Prague a young man in a black Škoda car stopped for me. He was the first one to tell me that 'something's wrong'. It was not until I came to the halls of residence that I began to comprehend the impact of it all by seeing the students announcing their strike action. The first sensation was fear, but you get over it in a crowd. This is how our new life began. The majority of the people expressed their support for us. They had had enough of the almighty Communist Party, the only party with the only truth and no other, and also because we were their children.

After the breaking of the information barrier on radio and TV, it was obvious that you could not stop the avalanche. We were united because we all wanted one thing: the removal of the old regime in which belonging to the party and possessing a red identity card meant more than real abilities. I was the hundred and fifty thousandth in the crowd that shouted in Wenceslas Square: 'We have had enough!'

Access to information was easy. We could find out about everything at the university. We, the medical students, performed mainly a medical service and I remember very well that I helped at least three people. They were mainly minor forms of collapse that were easy to deal with. The activity of the students was not chaotic. Our programme was well worked out and all the faculties co-operated with each other. Information on how we were received, how students were accepted in the industrial enterprises, which schools and colleges were on strike together with us, on the results of talks between our representatives, the representatives of the Civic Forum and officials from the government, all that was at the beginning available only at the university students' headquarters.

I don't know what others at that time hoped for, but my wish was for free elections and on the basis of that the creation of a real picture of the diversified political forces that exist. The winning parties would have the support of the majority and as such be able to move things in our country a bit further and faster forward.

And today? The victorious movement has split into three parties. Instead of the old cadre screening, the new political 'cleansing' process – a wonderful example of how to liquidate the oppositional elite. Instead of genuine price increases, 'liberalisation' – everything is at least twice as expensive whilst the quality remains the same. The course of our political life has turned 180 degrees to the west, accompanied by lots of primitive anti-communism. The last time the now-famous tank was painted pink, it was done by the members of parliament, deliberately transgressing their own laws. The prisoners given amnesty now murder and steal.

It all seemed to start with the Civic Forum's demagogic propaganda of the type 'If you don't vote for us, the Communists will get in.' That was in the elections with 51 per cent of the votes. I didn't like that. There was also a breach of the electoral legislation with the Bartončík affair, but that was passed over very quietly. It happened 48 hours before the elections when no one was supposed to have embarked on any action detrimental to the pre-election process. In the case of Bartončík, a member of parliament, there was an infringement. He was accused of collaboration with the StB, the secret police.

President Havel shook hands with Kurt Waldheim, and our biggest worry is the removal of the Soviet troops. Parliament, instead of addressing legislation on the economy, spends time on restitutions. We evaluate what happened in the past, how badly we treated the Sudeten Germans, but not enough is done for those like young families, pensioners or the socially deprived so that they don't have to live in total destitution. Apart from the freedom of the press, which is now subject to 22 per cent VAT, and the opportunity to travel (even if not many can afford it), little has been done for the people. I think that many people also grumble because the only thing that MPs have managed to agree on up to now is their salaries. They voted to award themselves 13,000 crowns before they had even achieved anything. They can afford it. They cannot be recalled. And when something goes wrong, blame is put on the heritage of the past regime.

Simply, I don't think I would put this 'velvet' of ours on once again. Incidentally, the events of 17 November have still not been fully investigated.

POLAND

A country of drama. A country that always fought for its identity, its borders, its independence. A country that lost six million of its people in the Second World War. A country that has a long history of working-class radicalism, culminating in 1980 with the recognition of the ten-million-strong Solidarnosc (Solidarity) movement. 1981 martial law was a return to the dark ages as far as its population was concerned. There was no outside invasion, (though the Warsaw Pact troops had their military manoeuvres on Polish soil not long before) but the internal army intervened. What followed were, on the one hand, systematic attacks on all the activists, while at the same time, there was liberalisation of travel and later on the lifting of censorship on cultural expression. This was the Polish 1980s: divide and rule. From a mass movement, Solidarnosc too became split, and by the end of the 80s its more vocal section proclaimed the road to a market economy. In 1989 a round-table debate took place between the government under Jaruzelski and Solidarnosc, resulting in the first non-Communist government in Eastern Europe. Poland proclaimed itself a republic in December 1989. A series of harsh economic reforms followed, with inflation growing by 640 per cent between 1988 and

1989, and a 30 per cent drop in the standard of living; unemployment hit 11 per cent. The Catholic Church changed from a radicalising influence into a restraining one, putting a stop to abortion laws and the like, and in the recent 1991 elections it has had an unprecedented influence on the people, who say they go to their priest before they go to the ballot box. Lech Walesa, who rose from shipyard worker to become President in 1990, has fallen out with some of his earlier Solidarnosc allies, is reputed to be dictatorial and unpredictable, and has declared the new era in Poland to be the 'Third Polish Republic'.

Population: 37.5 million
Capital: Warsaw

1918	– First independent Polish state since 1795.
1939	– September: Hitler's invasion; the Soviet army enters from the East and Poland is carved up between the two forces. Polish government in exile.
1944	– Warsaw uprising, followed by Hitler's virtual destruction of the city.
1945	– Liberated by the Red Army.
1947	– Elections widely regarded as rigged to give 80 per cent votes to the pro-Moscow Polish Workers' Party (PWP).
1948	– Gomulka, leader of PWP, removed and replaced in 1949 by B. Bierut, Stalin's nominee.
1956	– Poznan's uprising (53 dead recorded) against the falling living standards. Gomulka returns. November – legalisation of workers' councils; Attempts at reform and decentralisation.
1970–1	– Price rises and new wave of uprisings in the

Baltic region (300 dead recorded). Gomulka deposed.

1971 – Gierek in power; price freeze, consumerism financed through foreign borrowing.

1980 – Emergence of the first independent trade union, Solidarnosc; new price increases; a wave of strikes throughout the country; Lech Walesa presents Gierek with 21 demands. Solidarnosc has ten million members. The Catholic Church emerges as a political force. Gierek replaced by Kania in September.

1981 – General Jaruzelski takes power; general strike declared in March; martial law imposed in December; Solidarnosc suspended.

1983 – Martial law withdrawn.

1984 – Father Popieluszko murdered by the state security.

1988 – 'Round-table' talks take place; new constitution declared; Solidarnosc legalised; landslide victory for Solidarnosc in June elections. August – first non-Communist government under T. Mazowiecki.

1990 – L. Walesa elected President; wave of unemployment and hyperinflation.

1991 – First free elections for fifty years – the population splits its vote between Solidarnosc and the ex-Communists; only 40 per cent vote.

Ingelin Blix, aged 17, Gdynia

THE NIGHTMARE OF THE MARTIAL LAW

13 December 1981. I was only seven and did not understand many things going on around me but the memories of that Sunday morning have stayed for ever in my mind.

I woke up earlier than usual. That was caused by my parents' rushing around before their trip to Sweden. My younger sister and I usually went with them but in winter our parents were not particularly keen on taking us. Those trips didn't last long; their main aim was to supply the house with indispensable articles nearly inaccessible in our shops. My mother quite easily convinced me to stay at home with my sister and grandmother, saying she was going to ask Swedish Santa Claus for Christmas presents for us. Polish toyshops didn't thrill me much; they had very little to offer, unlike Swedish ones. I knew that my parents' every trip enlarged my toy collection, which in turn enlarged the circle of friends who flocked to admire my belongings.

My father is a Norwegian, which made my parents' foreign trips relatively easy. It enabled them not only to see the family but provided us with goods which were in short supply in our shops, mainly food and children's clothing. My father was then working as an electrician for a Norwegian shipping company, T. Klaveness & Co. He had three months' leave. Having already been a few weeks at home his intention was to stay for Christmas with us. His temporary visa was expiring just before the holidays, and my parents also wanted to extend my father's visa in the consulate in Malmö. He had to wait for a few years for a resident's visa and was granted it the following June. My parents were to take a night ferry from Swinoujscie on 13 December 1981. We were all waiting for my uncle from Gdańsk to arrive. He had promised to help grandmother with domestic duties, especially taking our lively dog for a walk. We lived in Gdynia so to get to Swinoujscie on time my parents had to leave in the afternoon. We were all very anxious for our usually very reliable uncle to arrive. I wasn't particularly concerned about the atmosphere at home. I was more upset that the television didn't seem to work so I couldn't watch Sunday children's television. My mother tried to cheer me up, saying that it might be a temporary breakdown of the transmitter. But there was another breakdown – of the telephone; my mother tried in vain to get through to Gdańsk. All of that made us think!

The mystery was cleared up when we made another attempt to switch the TV on. Martial law. I didn't know what it was about. My parents weren't sure either what the imposition of martial law meant. The Polish equivalent of that term as opposed to that in English implies more war than law. To clear up the situation my parents went to the consulate agency in Gdynia. They weren't given any precise information there either. My mother decided not to go abroad. However, it turned out later that she wouldn't be able to cross the border with her Polish passport anyway. Polish borders were closed to Poles. My father was determined to stay with us. But there was his visa, which was about to expire. The passport office in Gdańsk refused to deal with this. It was announced that going in and out of the country would be stopped. I strongly suspected that rich Swedish Santa Claus wouldn't visit us that year. And that came true.

My father had to leave Poland; he took the last ferry from

Gdańsk. We were left alone, not certain what to do and not being able to get in touch with him. There was a complete blockade of domestic and international telephone calls, and censorship of correspondence. In the streets many militia patrols appeared.

A few months later, in April, Father managed to get in touch with us. We learned that he had spent the Christmas of 1981 as the only guest of the Carlton Hotel in Oslo, sitting down to a Christmas Eve supper prepared by the only member of the staff there that day. He had left Gdańsk on 20 December on the *Silesia* ferry. Among the few passengers aboard was an official from the Gdynia consulate leaving Poland with his family. The ferry's route was to Nynashamn. It was diverted to Helsinki to meet a large group of journalists awaiting the passengers. My father managed to get in touch with his shipping company in Oslo, who then arranged a ticket for his further journey. The Polish embassy in Oslo promised to inform my father when the blockade would be lifted. He received that information in the following April while he was on his way to the United States. The enforced separation of loved ones affected many Polish families where mothers and fathers were taken away from their children. That was called internment.

Beata Pyka, aged 20, Ryzowka

MERCIFUL LORD, WE NEED YOUR HELP!

My name is Beata Pyka. I am twenty years old and a first-year pedagogy student in Cracow. I was born in the southern Polish city of Nowy Targ. I live in a village called Ryzowka. I am very fond of this place, which is surrounded from all sides by evergreen woods. The villagers are kind, warm hearted and broad minded. They all make up one big family. And indeed, the truth of the matter is that they are all related to one another.

It is not easy for me to recall the events leading up to 1980. However, I do remember the year 1980 itself. It was a special year both for my family and my country. On 13 May in St Peter's Square in Rome there was an assassination attempt on Pope John Paul II. On 28 May there was the death of the Polish Primate of the Millennium, Cardinal Stefan Wyszynski. The August of that year electrified the world with a wave of strikes which swept across the country. On 9 October my thirty-eight-year-old father died, leaving a thirty-two-year-old wife, a three-year-old son and a nine-year-old myself. His death shook the very foundations of our family and left a deep wound which took a long time to heal. The wound was reopened on the night of 13 December, the never-to-be-forgotten night of martial law. I spent that night with my mother on a train. We were returning from the city of Lodz, where we had spent some time with our relatives. I distinctly remember that during our stay there the adults were all keyed up about what was happening in the country. Of course, the momentous political events meant nothing to me. I was nine years old and my interests centred on toys, games and the glossy colourful books belonging to my relative. I got an inkling of the world outside at the central railway station in Lodz when I realised on what train I would have to spend the night. It was not at all like an inter-city train. I thought, however, that it would not do me too much harm to spend an overnight journey with thirty people in a single compartment once in a lifetime. I did not expect anything ominous to happen. I went to sleep peacefully.

When I woke up about 1 a.m. I saw a man sitting next to us. He was dressed in a black coat, a black hat and had a black briefcase. There was a pile of papers in it. He kept looking through them. He seemed very restless and cast furtive glances around him as if he was afraid of something or somebody. The fellow passengers all felt apprehensive about his presence. They must have been afraid of him. The man in black evidently realised this as he told those present to set their minds at rest – he had no desire to harm them in any way. He tried to speak calmly yet his voice trembled. It flitted through my mind that he was an escaped prisoner, a fugitive from justice. But whatever did he have his papers for? The man in black got off a few stations after Cracow and we were all relieved when he went.

We were back home at four in the morning. Feeling thoroughly exhausted after the long journey I went straight to bed. At seven I was aroused by my grandfather's anxious voice: 'You are asleep while Poland is in a state of war.' I did not quite understand what he meant. It was calm and peaceful outside and there were no signs of war that I could see. Since it was a Sunday my mother, my brother and I went to church. And there again, the priest celebrating Mass spoke about martial law and offered prayers for the restoration of a free Poland, for the imprisoned so that God would strengthen in them the spirit of faith and hope. At the end of the service the congregation – simple peasants – rose in a mood of hope and defiance to sing the Polish religious anthem, 'Before your altars we beseech you great God by the power of your grace return a free homeland to us'. These deeply moving strains not only resounded in churches throughout the whole of the country but were also often heard out of doors.

At 9 a.m. on Sundays I always watched the 'Good morning, kids' programme. On this Sunday the 13th I turned on the TV only to see the stern and unsympathetic face of General Jaruzelski. 'What is this guy doing? Why isn't the children's programme on?' I asked fretfully, 'It's after nine.' It was only when my mother started thinking aloud that I 'twigged': the man in black we had travelled with was a Solidarity activist who had just slipped from police hands. The black briefcase had contained very important papers which the commies were more than anxious to seize. I was quite sure that had been the case. 'But the man in black was frightened,' I thought. It seemed ironic to me that adults should get scared. Yet the full significance of the events that had taken place escaped me.

After that the atmosphere at home became even gloomier than after my father's death. Fear, despondency and despair filled our day-to-day life. Night curfew, 300 per cent price rises, rationing of basic foodstuffs such as sugar, flour, butter, meat and sweets ... The contents of my mother's shopping bag grew less every day. Things reached a point when she started bringing bread only; most of the other staple food had become virtually unavailable. I cannot forget her face – pensive and careworn, it expressed all the love and frustration of a mother who knew she could not satisfy her children's most pressing needs. She tried so hard to make up to us for the loss of our father and the dramatic drop in our living standards, and yet she knew it was impossible.

The traditional Christmas Eve supper that year was a feast of sorrow and tears, not of laughter and rejoicing. An ominous silence hung over the table and we were unable to break it.

The following year was punctuated by 'falls' and 'rises'; it was a time of death and rebirth. Needless to say, the vast majority of people were wrapped up in their own affairs. They devoted all their energies to the art of survival in an economy crippled by mismanagement, inefficiency and chronic shortages. Those who had contacts managed to live quite comfortably. They bought things cheap and resold them at a profit. Black marketeers were the ones who called the shots. Less 'enterprising' individuals, people like ourselves, were forced to tighten their belts. Some grew rich, others suffered from poverty, in accordance with the saying 'As you make your bed, so you must lie upon it.' Things were far from easy where we lived, but perhaps they were not as bad as in the cities, where the most basic things had to be purchased. In the country there was milk, from which one could make cheese and butter, there was grain, which could be milled and made into bread, there were vegetables and potatoes. We were more fortunate than city-dwellers in another sense, too. We were mercifully spared the sight of tanks, armoured personnel carriers and the universally hated 'Zomo' riot police. But, of course, we were at the same time denied access to facts and treated to a false picture of reality by the strictly censored media. The scanty news that did reach us came through Radio Free Europe. We listened to it with avidity and later exchanged snippets of information in conspiratorial whispers. There were very few people that could be wholeheartedly trusted. Almost anybody could have turned out to be an informer. It came to me as some consolation that Father had not lived to see those dark moments of our country's history.

The subsequent years, as I see them now, were truly kaleidoscopic, and the events they gave birth to truly momentous: the Holy Father's visit to Poland in June 1983, the lifting of martial law, the awarding of the Nobel Peace prize to Lech Walesa, the assassination of Father Jerzy Popieluszko by the Polish secret service, an amnesty for political prisoners, new price rises, another wave of labour unrest, the 'round table', semi-free elections, new price rises, the appointment of Tadeusz Mazowiecki, the first non-Communist Prime Minister after the Second World War, the election of Lech Walesa as President.

Has the situation in our country improved? Many people cannot help asking themselves this question now that the old order has crumbled. Some answer it in the affirmative, others in the negative.

The hope and enthusiasm that lent us wings and inspired us to believe that great progress was within our reach seem to be evaporating. What is the use of the brightly lit, glittering shop windows and shops filled with beautifully packaged goods if they are foreign imports? They gladden the eye of the consumer, but we country folk realise only too well that they were not produced in our country. The butter, margarine, cheeses, yoghurts and tinned food were all imported. What shall we do with the homegrown food? Destroy it? But my mountain folk cannot bring themselves to do this, so they give away milk and meat for ridiculously low prices.

My relatives working in industry see the same thing. They say that there is no demand for Polish-made products and – if this trend is not reversed – all companies and factories will go bankrupt, leaving millions of people without work. Massive unemployment is bound to lead to poverty and crime. What kind of country will we live in if things do not change?

Yet, despite all this, we have not lost heart. We trust in God and are hoping for better times. We think that many sacrifices will have to be made, further self-denial will have to be practised and much determination will have to be shown in pursuit of new solutions if the country is to be pulled out of its deep crisis. Mountain folk say that everyone should start with themselves and that they should do their utmost to help others, not make use of them. They have the unshakeable conviction that their Heavenly Father will amply reward them for their present pains. And they put all their hearts and souls into the great hymn of faith and hope: 'Before your altars we beseech you, Merciful Lord, graciously bless our free homeland.'

Magdalena Pawelczyk, aged 20, Warsaw

A CHANGE – BUT WHAT NEXT?

A sickly, oppressive smell of tear gas. A muffled voice over a loudspeaker. The university gate is closed. Outside a number of stone-faced policemen standing in a long row. Banners hanging from all the windows. Someone cries 'Down with the Communists' and 'Jaruzelski must retire'. The first stone hits the gate.

It was early spring 1989 and I was about to complete the first year of my university studies. The academic year of 1988–9 was more of a political campaign – the angry young people of Poland had proved that the year 1968 would not be forgotten. We wanted our voice to be heard amidst the hot political discussions. We were not to be left unnoticed – missing the fun of organising a strike or the excitement of being chased by the police.

But at that time back in 1989 there seemed to be more than just 'being against'; it looked as if for the first time we were finally allowed to be serious – knowing that our voice would not be suppressed by a gun, we were no longer in fear of being arrested for taking part in a street demonstration. This already came as a change.

Events, however, came faster than anyone could have expected. The first half of 1989 brought about the talks of the round table, the legalisation of the trade union Solidarnosc and finally the creation of new democratic government under Mazowiecki. The rapidity and the short period of time in which the changes came left almost no place for thought. We were swept by the wave of optimism which seemed to subdue the ever-present feeling of uncertainty. It was difficult not to believe in a better future – although we hardly knew what shape it would take.

We were all eager to welcome the good effects of the democratic changes but unfortunately not patient enough to face the chaos that accompanied those changes. Today as I look back upon the year 1989 I realise that no matter how disorganised Poland's transition might have been, we had at least the right to feel optimistic about the future.

We felt satisfied on hearing our dirty past criticised in the mass media. We were enthusiastic about the new 'solidarity'-born politicians who came to power. In less than a year we had gained what seemed to be unattainable – democracy. But have we really?

The year 1991 brings no answer to that question. The political scene is still far from stable. The recent upheaval in the Soviet Union and the determination of the hardliners have not increased our optimism, which was already scarce. I remember that on hearing of the coup in the Soviet Union all I could think of was an ugly overwhelming image of chaos and a feeling that this time there would be no escape.

Our democracy came from the Soviet Union – from Gorbachev. Although the changes in Poland were much quicker, the feeling of being dependent on our eastern neighbour was still very much present. If there was any attempt to re-establish communist rule in the USSR it was obvious that we might be in danger. Are we to allow the destruction of the year 1989? Have we not suffered enough since the time of partition?

Although Gorbachev is back in power now it seems that Poland is still on the alert. The coup had reminded us that beside dealing with our domestic problems we must not forget about our Eastern neighbour, who remains an ever-present danger.

Today as I recall 1989 and 1990 I realise that Poland has undergone more than just a transition from a communist to a democratic state: from a traditionally Catholic country we have turned into a religiously obsessed people. I am a born but not a practising Catholic. I have always had a great respect for the Catholic faith and for the Pope, believing him to be one of the greatest statesman of the twentieth century. But Poland seems to be moving too far; I personally do not object to the priests preaching on TV and Lech Walesa being present at every religious ceremony, but there are people who openly criticise such religious display. Throughout the centuries Poland was known as a country with extreme religious tolerance. Is this to be forgotten nowadays?

It is difficult to decide whether the intensified Catholicism in Poland comes from a real need for the good Christian values to be reborn, or whether it is a reaction to forty years of obligatory atheism. I am inclined to believe in the latter, and I hope we shall soon regain a normal, rational state of mind.

I do not hesitate to call the years 1989–91 the turning point in our modern history. The times before belong to the past and it seems to me that one day I may forget that I ever lived in a communist country. Today out of the slowly disappearing chaos there emerges hope for a normal, stable life. The young people of Poland have finally reached a time when they can find a purpose in life. We have been given a choice, and a vision of a better future. Western Europe is no longer a forbidden land and the word 'success' has become meaningful. The political situation does not really matter as long as we are able to earn real money – for the young generation has become business oriented, and for them 'career' is the key-word in life. Destiny means money. As I am no exception, I fully identify with the aspirations of the young Poles.

HUNGARY

Hungary gained its reputation as an affluent and liberal country of Eastern Europe in the 1970s. It traded with the west, it relaxed its grip on the opposition and on foreign travel. There was no street drama in 1989, no revolution, just a slow move towards a western-style economy. The old Communist Party of Hungary cunningly renamed itself the Hungarian Socialist Party and its leader for thirty years, János Kádar, was forced to resign. A powerfully placed group of ex-communists was reputedly setting up big business ventures with western companies. The country was poised to transform itself. It became again the Hungarian Republic in 1989. When Mrs Thatcher went to Budapest in 1990, she liked it. The city offers shopping with major credit cards; you have to go outside the centre or to the more rural parts of the country to find the deprivation that accompanies the affluence. There is growing poverty, particularly among children, increased incidence of ill-health and deteriorating child welfare. Homelessness has become a problem, unemployment is rising (above 5 per cent) and the 'second economy' still operates. In the latest elections in 1990 most people didn't bother to vote. The taxi drivers in Budapest threatened a major wave of strikes. It is business companies that are asked to help with social programmes. The transition can be called a revolution from above. Some young people, as you will see, find this depressing; others find room for manoeuvre.

Population: 10.7 million
Capital: Budapest

1918	– Declaration of Independence after the break-up of the Austro-Hungarian empire.
1918–19	– Proclaims itself a Soviet Republic but is crushed.
1920	– Reverts to a kingdom without a king.
1920s and 30s	– Allies itself with the Fascist regimes, first Mussolini's Italy, then Hitler's Germany.
1941	– Hungarian army joins Hitler in his attack on the USSR.
1945	– Pro-Nazi regime pushed out by the Red Army. Hungary remains under Soviet occupation. November elections give Communist Party only 17 per cent and the Smallholders Party almost 60 per cent of votes.
1947	– Communist Party emerges as the single largest party in the elections.
1949	– A new 'socialist' constitution. M. Rákosi, the Prime Minister, brings in rigid Stalinist practices.
1953	– Rákosi resigns under pressure; replaced by Imre Nagy.
1956	– October demonstrations in Budapest are met with police fire; this escalates into a full uprising crushed by Soviet invasion in November. Imre Nagy executed; a wave of terror follows under the new leadership of Janos Kádar.
1961	– Some relaxation of Kádar's policies.
1968	– Launching of the 'New Economic Mechanism'; this brings about increased consumerism.

1972
–3   – Some recentralisation.
1982 – Price increases.
1988 – Kádar forced to retire, replaced by K. Grosz.
1989 – Communist Party renames itself Hungarian Socialist Party; parliament votes to dissolve itself.
1990 – Multi-party elections. Hungarian Democratic Forum – the largest party in the government with Alliance of Free Democrats as the main rival.
1991 – Hungary embraces full-scale market economy.

Anonymous, brothers, aged 16 and 18, Budapest

IS THIS DEMOCRACY?

We met in front of the Porsche building, an affront to many Hungarians, in central Budapest. The two brothers were ready to talk before I even put any questions to them. We walked to a nearby café, sat outside in the autumn sun, and over Cokes talked for about two hours. The following is a transcript of what they had to say.

The Kádar years, were called the years of a 'soft dictatorship'. We didn't feel its oppression very much. We simply didn't care that there was no free press or democracy. In school we were told that capitalism is bad and that there are foreign agents, but we never believed in what was said. Some people describe Hungary during Kádarism as the most 'cheerful barracks' of the communist bloc. We were free to do what we wanted inside the country. There was private enterprise. This was a compromise. People were allowed to do their own thing at home whilst in foreign policy we were tied to the Soviet system. When it came to celebrating 17 November with marches and pioneer scarves, nobody took it seriously. We didn't really realise what was going on but at the same time we didn't believe in the system. Our opinion about politics was that on occasions of official celebration we had a day off school.

The change was gradual. When Kádar was removed in 1988 it was the first step. His removal was symbolic but no big drama. Oppositional parties had been forming for a long time. The change was like an overspill. There was no violence, no blood. People hoped that things would be better, more democratic. But we think it failed.

I think that the country is about to be a one-party dictatorship again. This is not official, of course. But the Hungarian Democratic Forum dominates the press, the media and politics. They complain that the press is not optimistic enough. They don't set out to create a dictatorship, but at the same time they are not changing their policies. What we have is new people but the same style of politics. The system seems to be the same, only the ideology is different. There is a strongly nationalistic element. The religion of communism has been replaced by Christian ideas. Mind you, the communists were never communists in the real sense of the word. They didn't believe in the ideals of communism, they never attempted to create a better community. They had no real values, it was just a mask. Perhaps it's similar with the Christian democrats.

During the elections of 1990 swastikas appeared on the walls. There were slogans like 'We blame the communists and the Jews for the past 40 years of mistakes.' This is 1,500-year-old stuff. Graffiti like this could be seen: ✡ = ☭ = $ People didn't know the exact meaning of what they were saying. There is a danger, a serious danger, but it's better now and it's not the whole truth.

One of the members of parliament, Imra Konya from the Hungarian Democratic Forum, wrote an essay some time ago giving his views of the next years of development here. It was completely anti-democratic. He said something like: 'The party should not follow the opinion of the majority. It's the supporting minority that should be followed.' He is influential, anti-democratic, there was public outcry. But the President is respected. He is a European man, though he has no real power. He is popular with the press. He comes from within the opposition.

But there are also good things. Western capital is interested in Hungary. People get the right idea about how to do business. The switch to the market economy means that prices are up, subsidies are out, our foreign debt is up. We don't have money to raise salaries. There is more poverty, unemployment. The factories are closing, there is inflation, beggars in the streets. Our parents are relatively OK, though. We will survive. Not all the problems are the faults of the system now; it began earlier.

I want to be a teacher and the prospect is potential poverty. The jobs in high schools are not very well paid. You have to do additional jobs, translations, private lessons to make ends meet. It's unpredictable what will happen. There is a danger of things turning bad. Maybe not.

We feel that Hungary is the western edge of Eastern Europe. It's better off than most. It's a one-nation country, there is no danger of clashes. Our neighbour, Romania, is in bad trouble. So is the Soviet Union. Empires cannot last for ever. When Gorbachev was removed this summer, people were afraid. All our achievements could disappear. The Soviet Union has a big influence on us. Without their oil and gas we would collapse. We still trade with them. They are the closest source of our raw materials. We should not cut these sources off just because of politics.

There are so many conflicts elsewhere – the Albanians, the Serbs, the Poles, the Latvians. We don't have the same problems in our country. The two million Hungarians in Romania for example don't have their own schools or language. The Romanians are worried that we may want our territory back. But the government is careful, the Prime Minister is responsible.

Compared with the other ex-communist countries, we are in a good position. But that's not enough. 1956 was a radical change. It was a chance to break away. After that, everything was gradual. It was the only way for us. Violence and blood does not bring about democracy. Except we had to wait for Gorbachev. We were let out of the fold. People don't want to hear about socialism any more. They have lived in misery. They are so angry with the past that they want to throw the whole thing out. But even now they have been promised things and not much has come true. Most people don't vote. They may think that America, for example, is a paradise. But we went there and saw poverty. It's a home of extremes: there is light and darkness; lots of money and lots of poverty; sharp boundaries.

Ourselves, we have about six quiet years ahead of us studying. We don't have to think about the future. We are somewhat protected. We shall see.

Anna Radnóti, aged 16, Budapest
NO CHANGE

A *transcript of a conversation in Budapest, October 1991.*

I don't think this revolution has changed very much. OK, my family now has more money. My father was unemployed before for the past ten years. It was political unemployment. He was a member of an organisation, they went on strike, he was kicked out. He was also an editor of a journal. Now he is an editor again, but of his own journal. He was unemployed because he was a member of the Free Democrats. It was quite hard. My mother worked and we lived with my grandmother. We didn't have much money. Now it's better in this way. In other ways not much has changed. There are more places for entertainment, that's all.

The revolution was not the main change. A year and a half ago I thought it would be something else. It has been shown that it is all the same. Now, it's called democracy, but it's the same. There are problems in the economy. There is a deep mess. I am a member of IDE, the Young Free Democrats. Not an active member, but because when I was a little girl my father took me everywhere to all the meetings and strikes. Many friends of ours are now in parliament as senators. Being a member can't change much, but I wanted to be a member of the Young Free Democrats. I thought that they could become the leading party. But it was just a dream. It would be as hard for them as it is for the present leading party. This country is going down. The first problem is the economy and then there is the culture.

There is still 5 per cent illiteracy. I can't see it getting any better for the next ten years. I have to change my thoughts. It would be good to see Hungary like other countries, say Austria. It is so close to us. Their life is better. That's the maximum I would like to see here. It's not democracy here now because the TV and the radio work for the leading party. So it can't be a democracy. When every newspaper is the same, it's not democracy. I have never lived in one, so I don't really know.

When things started changing I was very excited. It was a real historical event. I was also excited when there was the coup in the Soviet Union this year. It's very good to live in history. In the last forty years there have been no historical events. I was happy not about the coup, that was wrong, but then Yeltsin and Gorbachev came back. Though I don't think Gorbachev has much power now it was good to see that something had changed there. When the coup failed, it was a happy moment. But it was hard for the Soviet Union and for the Soviet people. We are so close. It's good for some of the republics like the Baltics, but not so good for others, like the southern parts. They have no economy.

And what is communism to me? I don't know what it means. I was only fourteen when things started changing. In those fourteen years it was not so good. Now, I am happy. But it's my father and grandmother who can turn around and blame the system; they were adults. But me, I was only a child. It was not much different from today. The year 1956 probably meant the same thing to my father as the current revolution means to me. They didn't want to do anything, they couldn't. They were ten years old. But I don't think they have any bitter feelings.

Poland was the first, with Hungary, to have these revolutions. Poland is worse because we have more changes. They say that they have democracy. I think we have more, though

I don't know what democracy means precisely. The collapse of the Berlin Wall was good. But the East Germans have the same feelings as in Hungary. West Germany wants them to be a part of them but they don't have the same level of economy. It will be bad.

My father's aunt lives in Romania, in Transylvania. We sometimes go there and she stays here for the whole of the winter. There is no coal, no water. She is my grandmother's sister. She comes from December to April to live here through the winter. She says that it's really difficult. It was hard to live under Ceaucescu, but it's as hard to live there now, maybe even harder. There was meat in the shops in Romania after Ceaucescu went, and the Hungarians went there and bought lots of stuff. It was cheaper. They have the same problems now. Nothing has been solved. There is anger. The Hungarians living there stay because it's their home, but I think they would like to join Hungary. But it's no good to think of a 'big Hungary', of expansion. Some Romanians think that though. They are afraid of the present regime. The feelings don't go away.

I will not go into politics. I don't know what my future will be. Maybe I will be a history teacher. I would like to live in a better world. I have friends who want to do something. I don't feel any loyalty really. It means a lot to me to be here, but I won't be the one to take any active part. When I joined the Young Free Democrats I thought that I could do things. I will sign things and such like, but otherwise, no.

There is little change in my life between past and present. There are possibilities, especially travel. I have already visited ten countries: I have seen a lot. We started travelling in 1986.

One of my best friends decided to join the Young Free Democrats. But she is tired of the government, I am tired of it. It's the government's fault that we feel tired. Other of our friends are not interested in politics. They are only interested in their lives. I am open-minded, I read newspapers, watch TV, and so on, but lots don't. If there is a new government it will be harder for them than the present government, because people have lost interest.

DOES ONE NEED TO BELONG?

A *transcript of a group discussion with Péter Vági, Olívia Thuma, János Ungár, Eszter Vági and Mazsi Barna, aged 16–19, Budapest, October 1991.*

Péter: I think that the present situation looks like a restructuring back to the 1920s and 1930s. The whole of the European right wing is strengthening and the left is weakening. But I am impressed by the speed of things in our part of the world. It's unbelievable that such radical changes could take place in a relatively small region with such lasting impact.

Olívia: These changes were sudden; you could see them in my family and school. They opened up new chances. Materially, things are potentially better. My father works in publishing, and my mother, who is Polish, in the Polish cultural centre. I go to a Polish school which has improved, we have new books, etc. Personal changes in the school are good, like new teachers, who otherwise would not have had the right to teach.

János: I am optimistic about the political development here. There is a move towards democracy and this is a good trend. The multi-party system safeguards the functioning of democracy. It's important that we have the right of free speech. There are sometimes radical and undesirable offshoots of that, but on the whole it's OK. There are no major changes in my family and personal life. The real changes are in the rights and feelings of the people.

Eszter: There is ambivalence. Bad and good things

happened. But I am cautious about my final opinion because I don't have an overall view of all the tendencies. In my school there were important and good changes. History teaching is different now, lots of things are discussed that were not before. On a more general social level the radical changes led to a manifestation of massive social differences. You can see that there are wealthy people and there is poverty; great poverty that was unimaginable before. You can't go through the city centre without meeting beggars, and you wouldn't have seen them before.

Mazsi: There were important changes in my family life. My mother is a school director, and could not have done the job without being a member of the Communist Party and other organisations. What I remember best as a significant change was the funeral of Imre Nagy in June 1989. Not only because it's generally seen as a turning point, but because of my mother's experience. She, for the first time, admitted some sort of guilty feelings, though personally she was not guilty or responsible. The funeral was broadcast live on TV and my mother was deeply depressed and crying. She asked me not to listen to loud music and was shocked; she said she could not imagine how she could belong to a party that did these things, though she didn't know what the party really did. But she felt guilty. It may be that my mother never belonged to the Communist Party in a true sense. It didn't take long before she was fired because of her commitment to reform and involvement in political changes. Now she is not a member of any of the parties. People in the old system had a need to belong to something, and the Communist Party was really the only possibility. Many of the members were not really responsible but just had this need.

Eszter: I want to add that it is a big task now to think through these experiences about how people believed in communism and their need to belong as committed members. In our family, my grandmother belonged to the Communist Party. She was very active in it. My grandfather fought for the unification of the Social Democrats and the Communist Party after 1945. He belonged to the Social Democrats who later joined. But he was much more reserved. Grandmother was active, she was younger. The regime made it possible for her to be very socially mobile. She came from a low class and became an intellectual. So her relationship to the whole thing was very different. But one of her daughters is in the centre as an activist for the Free Democrats now. Granny then had an insight into both parties and how they worked, and we had interesting discussions before the elections. It was funny how she thought about it all and decided that there are individual choices and party choices. So when it came to the elections, she supported – as a party – the reformed Communist Party but the individual member she went to vote for was from the Free Democrats. She really found it important to express that a combination was what she would like to see.

It is unjust and confusing now that the people who belonged to the Communist Party are put on trial and blamed for all the things that happened. It was not just what Mazsi said, that people wanted to belong, but also some of the ideas were attractive. People felt that they could identify with them. With the changes now, it's confusing. Many of the values that were emphasised for so long are no longer discussed, and the whole agenda of public discussion has changed. The old values are suppressed and those values that could not be discussed for so long come to the surface.

Mazsi: In the short run I am more pessimistic than optimistic, because I think that what the government is doing is disastrous. I am very critical, and I think that the whole political setting should be criticised. In the long run, though, I have to be optimistic for reasons of self-defence. I don't want to leave; I want to remain here, so I need to be optimistic. What gives me a very bad feeling is that as a person you have to feel ashamed for your leaders. Nobody could be trusted, and I don't feel I can support anyone.

Péter: I think what is bad is that democracy here didn't follow a healthy path. It happened in the opposite way to what had been decided. I feel that what's unhealthy and dangerous, though somehow natural, is that there is no new structure of trade unions. They should have developed as protective organisations against direct politics and to protect work, to develop new values. The absence of trade unions is a danger. Those that have developed are weak and formal, and don't have the strength and values useful for long-term functioning. Another very unhealthy thing is that the new political power has taken over the monopoly of information and control of the media. The problem is that financial and moral power should not be so concentrated in the top leadership as it is now. They have all the means in their hands. There are no independent newspapers and no independent newscasting. If that remains it will be dangerous for democracy. The third danger is the growing political demagogy. Our march to Europe is overemphasised. Since joining the EC is regarded as the first priority, instead of step-by-step gradual development, it means that things that need developing and are required in our society can't develop, and only the requirements of the EC will be met. This may even destroy some parts of our social development, and is dangerous. There will be no organic building of what we need. What people find the most irritating is how the new power misuses this period: they blame the old regime. But what goes on is standardisation of power building now. The reprivatisation and change in values is dangerous, particularly the way the Church is handled.

Mazsi: I want to emphasise that I don't agree with Péter.

The most dangerous and disastrous thing about the media is that they are unreliable. On the other hand, I don't think I could have kept my Jewish identity in the old regime. Now, it's important that Jewish people can have their holidays, etc. The police are now visible around the synagogues to protect people. It's a two-sided thing. They are there to protect but of course it's also a sign that anti-Semitism is still there. The situation is full of tension. But I think it's good that it is now an open thing that the state declares its support for the Jews, and doesn't go back to the old anti-Semitism. In my view, the Jewish question is tricky. But we have the gypsies and racism. They can be blamed for being dirty and having too many children, but when the country goes down and there is poverty, the Jews are in more danger, and blamed for their wealth. In the long run then anti-Semitism is dangerous because it can't be seen so easily. But of course, the gypsy families suffer. There was a gypsy family on the tram and I was the only one who didn't move away. An argument started.

Péter: I regard racism against the gypsies as more dangerous than anti-Semitism. It's of secondary importance in the hierarchy because the Jews have their political formations and self-protective groups to fight back. The Jews are represented in Parliament and politics, the gypsies are not. To add to this, gypsies are the biggest minority, some 5 to 8 per cent of the population, and their protection is minimal. Jews are protected officially, and they have their own culture that is being revitalised. You can take Hebrew classes, but there is no support for gypsy culture. Their schools are closed down and there are many disadvantages for gypsy children. That's what's dangerous.

Mazsi: We agree that in the short run the gypsies are endangered the most, but if the right gets organised, anti-Semitism could grow. The search for scapegoats is going on all the time. At the moment it's the communists, but it's dangerous that it is going on.

Eszter: I want to say that the handling of religion in general is ambiguous. I feel it's overemphasised. There is a growing interest in religion but what's difficult for our age group is that our dilemmas about the world increase. They have introduced compulsory religion in schools, not all, but many. We are confused.

Péter: My primary school was quite conservative, with its pioneer movement that we were forced to join. Without the changes, this would not have altered.

Mazsi: My own story goes back to 1989 when we went to East Germany for holidays. We were the only Hungarians. The Germans felt that the Hungarians were already liberated, and although they thought that changes should take place, they didn't think it would happen. They were under pressure and controlled.

Péter: The truth is that as the Soviet Union fell apart, the whole system falls apart. What remains is just the parts. It's interesting to see how the second biggest power falls apart. It's not reversible. But we could never have imagined that it would happen.

János: Hungary is comparatively the most stable. Relatively speaking, when we look at the other countries. Although there are internal conflicts, to the outside world we appear united.

Péter: This stability is an outcome of the lack of oppositional power. It's a weakness. Last year, the taxi drivers' strike could have shaken the country. It's an apparent stability, not a real one.

Mazsi: This country is preoccupied with internal affairs now. Before, we knew more about the world. I think that the real changes have not started in some countries yet, like Yugoslavia or Romania, or the Slovaks in Czechoslovakia. Pesonally, I feel excited about what's going on in the Soviet

Union. They need help but also they have to fight seventy years of history. The figures of their history have to be faced; life for generations was overshadowed by them. They have the bravest and the hardest task. Hungary in that context has a better living standard, and conflicts elsewhere are more serious. Though the country has become a meeting place for other immigrants, there are problems. My mother for example had a strange experience when a young man from Transylvania came and wanted to study here. He asked for help. The university wouldn't accept him without a job certificate. Our government criticises the Czechs and the Yugoslavs, but in real life they act the same.

Eszter: What did communism mean to us? I think the worst thing was its demagogy. It was very intensive. In political and economic terms it was a failure, a mistake, though the idea is attractive, good but unrealistic. It's true what is being said: 'The best communism or socialism can be realised under capitalist conditions.' Many issues could not be discussed in the past, or you had just one opinion presented. The good side, in my experience, was that the social and material differences were smaller then than now. The whole order of values was clearer, it was a crystallised set of values. Now it's more confused. Though the multi-party system offers choice, many people have lost orientation. Life used to be easier, and although I was critical of the past, people had clearer orientation then.

János: Before the changes, I was not interested in politics. What I know about the old system is that it was a one-party system which created lots of disadvantages. If you wanted to take up a job, you had to join the party. It's more important that people did good work, but now it's unjust that they are criticised for their membership. Some of the inbuilt failures in the old system were no free press, etc. But it has to be kept in mind that Kádar tried to balance things. The Communist Party didn't go against the people.

The peace kept in the country was important. There was a satisfactory living standard, with less deprivation than now. I think that even in the old system people who wanted to reach high positions and have a good future could do that. I think it's unjust that people who left the country in masses in 1956 and are now coming back are given better positions than those who have suffered, the people who stayed.

Péter: I think it was quite a stable system in the past, though stability was weakened after 1956. The question can be raised: if it was stable why did it break down? The reasons can be found outside the system. It was the inbuilt dysfunctions that led to the revolution. The most important good aspect of the past was its stability. By the end of its existence, that system had managed to develop real politicians. Its stability was embedded in the ability to control nearly everything. Since it could control everything, anything oppositional had to develop underground. Control was exercised in a dictatorial way, yes. But if one looks, democracy can be weakened and questioned more easily. It can be weakened because with the freedom to express all ideas, extreme right-wing views can be voiced. Many democracies are endangered because of social differences and discontent. Democracies now are being disrupted. The old system could control dangerous radical movements. Though the control was too much, some of it is necessary. If the world at large had recognised these advantages, something could have been done. Our countries have been ghettoised. If other countries show more interest, the dictatorial way will not go so far. I think the causes of the collapse of democracy and socialism are different. Socialism and its ideas were not in accordance with each other. Sometimes it happens to democratic systems too, where democratic principles and ideas do not match reality.

Mazsi: I thought about why we responded in this way. It's a difficult question, to assess communism. Relatively speaking, Kádar's period meant less material differences: less wealth but also less poverty. The price was an inefficient economy. The state didn't allow efficiency. That's coming to the surface now. I travelled recently and listened to two women arguing that they had a better life before, that they could go to the opera and such like. They don't see what it cost. So I think it's difficult to talk of good aspects. Everything had a bad side, anything good was overshadowed. The last communist government was better, the one in 1988. The bad things can be summarised more easily and are well known, for example the economy. What is problematic is that there are generations that have been brought up in the old regime. For me, the old regime started in the 1970s and the changes began in the late seventies and the eighties. That was the road to transition. Kádar could not step down, he had to be brought down. My generation is aware of the fifties and its camps, the defeat of 1956. These disasters were part of the old system. All in all, however, individuals should not be labelled as responsible and witch-hunted. It was the system. It's more important to think how that system worked and have a deeper understanding.

Olívia: I was most irritated by the mass organisations – the pioneers, the Communist Party. Everyone had to join. Even if you wanted to express other sentiments like patriotism, you had to join. It should be a choice. People were much more restricted. You couldn't do what you wanted; you had to do what was required. Now, alternatives are opened. People didn't have freedom of opinion. My grandma was deeply religious but had to keep it secret. At school we never had any influence on matters that concerned us.

Péter: It's not a good thing that each generation cannot change the system. The present over-politicised situation is a result of that.

Eszter: The generation that has now come to power, the

generation of our parents, was born during or before the war. Their political experience came as a result of the war. Nostalgia for pre-war times comes from that. My generation experiences things in a more direct way.

Mazsi: I still think it's ambivalent to say that our parents' generation contributed to the old system. They also brought about the new changes. They can't be criticised as such.

János: Generations can't be criticised, only individuals can.

Péter: I disagree. Generations can have a historical role. Sharing it with a younger generation would help. Now, I feel that the important thing for me is to go to university. Do well.

Olívia: I would like to go to university, but I'm not sure what I'll do.

János: My idea is to enter business life, be an enterpreneur.

Eszter: I want to combine university with the theatre. And I want to lead a stable, normal family life without conflicts.

Mazsi: I shall learn English and other languages. It's important for any future work. I may study law with economics. I feel enthusiastic. With the booming enterprise culture, economic law is a steady career. Also, I would like to write in a journal, test myself, combine career, writing and normal family life.

OUR OVER-POLITICISED PAST

Transcript of a discussion with Péter Kolosi, Fruzsina Sánoor and Klara Dobrev, aged 19–20, Budapest, October 1991.

Péter: You will hear bad things. But we are going in a positive direction. There are dead ends, yes, but the main road is positive. Hungary was always ruled by other empires. The last forty years were better for us than the other East European countries. There was hard Stalinism but after 1956 it eased up. We were not as militarily important as the others. Kádár might have been the only one in the communist bloc who believed in communism. He wanted to give more to the people. He was keen to protect friendship with the USSR, but economically he gave a lot. People could travel, have cars. That is why Hungary didn't need to be so revolutionary as others. You didn't have such a strong dictatorship so the changes were not so fast.

Klara: There is lots of confused and complicated thinking. For example a public opinion poll revealed that the most popular party was the Socialist Party [the reformed Communist Party], but people didn't vote for them, they voted for the Hungarian Democratic Forum. They voted for change.

Fruzsina: The members of the government are not popular. They have to do unpopular things.

Péter: People are getting unpolitical. Everything was

over-politicised in the past. You couldn't go on the streets without being bombarded by something.

Klara: The last ten years we were discussing politics all the time.

Péter: We were the first lucky generation. My father was a member of the Communist Party. I like him but I hated communism. My mother was afraid I would not be accepted at the university, and thought I should join the Young Communist organisation. Father said, just do what you want.

Klara: I was the secretary of the Young Communists in our district. We had many discussions.

Péter: All that time it was not clear what was to come – another Stalin or new changes. We organised together [with Klara] though we were on opposite sides as far as our ideas were concerned. We started a new students' self-governing body to express our views. The headmistress was liberal, though strict. When we started thinking of a nationwide organisation, separate and in some ways in competition with the Young Communists, they gave us rooms and allowed us to print our material there. Of course, there was an advantage for them – they could read everything we said first without employing spies. We had big debates with the ministries and Department of Education and Culture. We were allowed to organise but we couldn't say anything to the CP. Pluralisation happened but they were not glad to see it. For example they didn't want to hear anything about celebrating '56.

Klara: We didn't have power. At fourteen you don't, but we organised camps and activities.

Péter: We had problems with the Students' Alliance and we wanted to have an international press conference. This was the first time we were stopped. We were told face to face by the Department of Education and Culture, nothing on paper, and the headmistress was called.

Klara: We may look like heroes now, but we didn't

realise we were the opposition. It was just normal to talk, to organise.

Péter: The Young Democrats [Fides] were formed five days later. The newspapers reported the banning of Fides. Our headmistress just warned us but didn't tell us to stop anything.

Klara: Once we organised a debate that was illegal. We invited an illegal oppositional organisation and were ready to argue against them. But when the speaker came, we listened, realised that he was right, and a new discussion began. We learned a lot.

Péter: It's interesting that the people from inside began to demolish the system.

Fruzsina: My parents were always against the system. I was not political. I have mixed feelings about the future. I don't like the way they do things now. They blame each other. They do things for their own interest. I am afraid. My parents were not members of the party, though my father actually was. They are angry, they still don't like the system now.

Klara: Power is now in the hands of historians, teachers, and people like that. They make mistakes. Not ideological ones but technocratic. They are in power but they are not specialists. All the experts were thrown out, there are not enough bureaucrats and technocrats. Most people are inexperienced.

Péter: In the past, you had to be a member of the Communist Party. I am optimistic because people now are coming into positions and can prove themselves if they are talented or not.

Klara: There were certain things that I believed in. Capitalism is not equal. I believed that the system was not so bad, though lots of it was very idealistic.

Péter: I don't want to be involved in politics any more. I did what I had to do. I am interested in the theatre. I want to be an actor.

Fruzsina: I study foreign trade, but am interested in history. I find the Second World War fascinating. It was a very important period. But I shall probably continue to do what I do now. It will give me a job.

Klara: I'm an economics student and study finance, banking and the stock market. And yes, I am interested in politics. I will come back to it. In high school I wanted to become president of the United Nations. I feel like a fish in water with politics.

Péter: I think that your Churchill was right. Western democracy may not be the best but you can't find anything better. I have friends in the west and they always say: your problems are nothing, ours are much worse. First you get the problems, then you look for change. Here, Grosz [reformed communist in 1986] wanted to change economics without changing politics. He was a Bolshevik. But now people have change and they are disappointed. The west was a dream for them. Nobody saw the problem. To have better economics, better democracy, you have to pay a price.

Klara: I am optimistic that Europe will be European, including Russia. I would like to see Europe without borders, with a free economy, unified, but preserving national characteristics. All countries should be equal, demilitarised, but strong enough to defend themselves. It's natural to want to become rich if you engage in business. But some say that if you are rich you are bad. Communism was when you didn't have too much. And the danger of the communists coming back? They are just a handful of seventy-year-olds.

Péter: In the past, rich people became rich because they engaged in illegal activities. The differences now, however, are much bigger. If you have any money, you can make more. It is important to build a strong social system to protect the weak. Hospitals are poor, so are the theatres. One day, I think, it will be possible.

THE SOVIET UNION

The country that has undergone massive changes, too massive to comprehend. From the first country to have a revolution in 1917 to a country that had one of the worst dictatorships under Stalin, to a country that stood as a political and ideological enemy of the west, to a country that has broken with its past, dismantled its own empire and let go of the satellite countries of Eastern Europe: all in less than eighty years! No wonder its people are in a state of shock, no wonder they have suffered beyond their endurance. Gorbachev came to power in 1985, after a series of top-level changes that included the death of the USSR's three leaders, Brezhnev, Andropov and Chernenko, baffling the Americans, whose foreign policy towards the Soviet Union was said to be reduced to shaking hands at funerals. Gorbachev was a man of action. He shifted his enemies to the sidelines, he led from the top. And despite the unsuccessful coup, and the dissolution of the old Union, he will remain the figurehead of the changes. He was not loved at home; quite the contrary. He has brought about unpopular measures during his reign, in particular an attack on some of the more outspoken republics, more stringent work discipline for the average person, and little in the shops. On the other hand, as a pragmatist he saw the opportunity and allowed its semi-free passage. The Union is broken, political loosening is on the agenda, the road to learning non-dictatorial ways of handling things may have begun. It's a country full of contradictions, with its own contradictory and complex past. There are others besides Gorbachev but we hear little of them; there are concerns ranging from nationalism, anti-Semitism and women protesting against conscription, to cries of: 'Our leaders have stopped listening to the people!' The old Soviet Union reflects the insularity of both east and west. Are we facing a new beginning? Are the people of the last remaining empire ready to be part of a new world, or do they need to settle their own scores first? I want to hear from its young people.

Population: 275 million
Capital: Moscow

1917	– Bolshevik revolution; establishment of the first socialist government.
1918 –20	– Civil war; period of war communism; western hostilities.
1921	– New Economic Policy of Lenin, allowing some private market activities; suppression of Kronstadt workers' revolt.
1924	– Lenin dies.
1926	– Stalin in power.
1929	– The first five-year economic plan, with forced collectivisation and industrialisation.
1934 –6	– The great purges; terror; suppression of opposition and of nationalities.

1941	– Invasion by Hitler.
1945–8	– End of the war and annexation of Eastern Europe.
1949	– Founding of Comecon.
1953	– Stalin dies; replaced by Khruschev.
1955	– Warsaw Pact formed in response to NATO.
1956	– Khruschev's 'secret' speech denouncing Stalin's crimes; invasion of Hungary.
1962	– Cuban missile crisis.
1964	– Khruschev deposed; succeeded by Brezhnev.
1965	– Attempts at economic reform ('Kosygin' reform); trials of dissidents.
1968	– Soviet-led invasion of Czechoslovakia.
1970s and 80s	– Years of stagnation.
1982	– Brezhnev dies; replaced by Andropov.
1984	– Andropov dies; replaced by Chernenko.
1985	– Chernenko dies. Gorbachev comes to power.
1986	– *Perestroika* and *glasnost* launched.
1987–8	– Spate of legislation on economic decentralisation; new voting laws.
1989	– Troops sent to Georgia (19 reported killed).
1990	– Troops sent to Lithuania.
1991	– Unsuccessful coup against Gorbachev; the parliament votes the Communist Party out of power; the Soviet Union changes its character with the independence of its fifteen republics. The old Soviet Union is replaced by The Commonwealth of Independent States.

Katya Kalinina, Moscow

THE RUSSIAN WHITE HOUSE UNDER BARRICADES

On the first day of the coup, 19 August 1991, I was in the country near Moscow where I stayed in our summer-house with my grandparents. I woke early that morning and was quite happy – it was so peaceful and lovely around, besides, I had ten more days on my own before the beginning of the next school year in September. I had breakfast and then decided to watch a morning pop-music programme on TV. But there was nothing on the third channel, which seemed very strange. It turned out that the only functioning channel was the first, the All-Union channel, and that was how I knew about the Extraordinary Committee and the alleged illness of Mikhail Gorbachev. I called Granny and Grandpa; we watched TV together but couldn't make out what it was all about. One thing was clear – we strongly disliked the members of the Committee and did not believe in Gorbachev's illness. Anyway, we were in confusion and I decided to go to Moscow to my parents. I called on a friend and we went to the neighbouring town to make a phone call to Moscow. On our way we noticed that although it was a warm day there were very few people in the streets. It seemed everything was too quiet, there was something unnatural about it. The queues to the phone booths were unusually long. My mother was not at home but my friend's mother said that the situation was extremely serious, that tanks and troops were entering Moscow and that we should stay in the country.

It was already afternoon when I was on my way back to Moscow. People in the train looked serious and reserved. When I met someone's eyes I felt secret sympathy and understanding. It was obvious that people were thinking in the same terms.

When I first saw the tanks I thought it was a movie. They proceeded at full speed along Sadovoye Koltso Street – a dark giant chain of them. I was shocked, I nearly burst into tears. At that moment I hated all the soldiers and the army in general.

Mother was at home and we had a talk. She said we had a dictatorship now, which everybody had been so afraid of lately. She was very pessimistic and said that life had lost any sense for her, that she had no hope and that parents, including herself, who gave birth to children in this country were criminals. She asked me to forgive her. I was really sorry for her. I was overwhelmed by resentment and weakness.

In the evening we watched the famous press conference. At first Mother and Father were worried but then they looked at each other and nearly laughed. Mother said: 'It can't possibly be serious. They lie so awkwardly.' After that conference she calmed down somewhat.

Next morning at about twelve we caught the illegal radio programme 'Echo of Moscow' and learned that the resistance was being organised everywhere, that several unsanctioned meetings had taken place, that many public figures openly opposed the Extraordinary Committee and that Yeltsyn called the members of the Committee state criminals.

It was impossible to stay at home with uneasy thoughts, so I went out with my friends. In the streets people surrounded the tanks and had stormy discussions with soldiers. Everybody asked them: 'Will you shoot at the people?' The soldiers were very young, most of them had nice and kind faces and they obviously did not quite understand what was happening. I was not afraid of them at all but their presence in the city offended me. We walked everywhere in the centre of Moscow – to Red Square, along the boulevards, to Tverskaya Street – and everywhere the picture was the same – tanks and soldiers near important buildings.

There were many people – several thousand – gathering near the Russian Parliament House, the White House. They were building barricades and preparing to spend the night there. Then it started raining and began to get dark; great anxiety was in the air. I knew that Mother was probably desperately worried about me, so I decided to return home.

Then came the crucial night. Mother and Father were very nervous but they thought it was useless to go against tanks. We could not sleep, we listened to the underground radio and waited – for something terrible to happen. Characteristically, there were no phone calls.

The night was really terrible. The rain was pouring down. At about two in the morning we heard the first gunshots, then more and more. A boy screamed in the night (he was probably standing by the window): 'They are shooting!' Mother was on the brink of a nervous breakdown – she thought hundreds of people had been killed. Father was deeply depressed.

In the morning Mother decided to go to the barricades to take some cigarettes to the people there and to learn the news. So we went to the White House. To our great relief the victims were not so numerous as we thought. There were tremendous crowds near the White House and in general it was not so frightening in the streets. It was much worse to stay at home. At the underground stations people expressed their indignation openly, there were numerous leaflets calling the Muscovites not to obey the Extraordinary Committee. The city was entirely different that morning.

People on the barricades seemed to be afraid of nothing. They were real heroes. They all had wonderful faces, I loved them all and felt so proud of them. In the morning of 21 August it became clear that the coup had failed, that the services of the Extraordinary Committee had been rejected.

Later that day we learned about the details of that frightening night – about the death of three boys, about Yeltsin, about soldiers taking Russia's side and so on. I was in the streets nearly all day. Russian tricolours were to be seen everywhere, they were on most of the tanks now.

At about three o'clock in the afternoon we heard that the notorious Committee had gone to the Crimea to Gorbachev. That meant victory! It made me really happy, I never loved my country and my people so much as at that time.

In the evening our life came back to normal, the greatest proof of which was that at last all the TV programmes were again functioning! On the morning of 22 August I watched the pop-music programme which I had failed to see on the 19th.

Our life returned to normal but I fully realise that it will never be the same now. I am glad that I am young. In spite of everything I believe in the future now.

Ludmila and Maria Ozerov, aged 16, Moscow

THE DAYS THAT SHOOK THE WORLD

We don't know all the details of those days. Some time will pass before we learn more. Maybe the events of those days will be described in history textbooks.

We were having a summer holiday in the country not far from Moscow. On 19 August early in the morning we heard the insistent ringing of the phone. A friend of our parents was calling from Moscow. He told us the news. It was announced that Gorbachev had become ill, that Vice-President Yanayev was carrying out the President's duties and a state of emergency had been introduced. The State Emergency Committee had been formed.

After this telephone conversation, the first words pronounced by all the members of our family almost simultaneously were: 'It's a military coup!'

We were very upset. My father left immediately and went to the newspaper where he worked. They held an illegal meeting and decided to publish their edition underground. The majority of the newspapers had been banned. We were very proud of the activities of our father's colleagues.

Later that terrible day, 'The Word to the People' from the Emergency Committee was being broadcast every hour. Tanks took position in Moscow streets and the next day a curfew was imposed. People didn't obey the Committee's orders. They had built barricades around the Russian parliament. Later, we watched everything on TV videos which had been made illegally by some brave journalists. We noticed one amazing thing – the faces of those who defended the Russian parliament were surprisingly beautiful. Or maybe, we thought, they became beautiful in those decisive moments.

The coup attempt had been suppressed very quickly, in three days. Gorbachev, who had been kept prisoner in his residence in the Crimea, was free again. Several days after the coup, we walked through the streets where the main events took place. Everything was quiet, but parts of the barricades still remained. We visited the place in one of the streets where the first blood was spilt. We knew that the funeral ceremony of the three killed young men would be broadcast on TV. We watched it the whole day. The men were of different nationalities – Russian, Ukrainian and a Jew. But they were united by their mutual aim: they were defending the freedom of our country. We could see the mournful faces of their mothers. The funeral music was sounding sorrowfully, the faces on the portraits of the killed men were beautiful . . . Life goes on. We, people, argue, love, hate . . . But no miracle can bring back the lives lost.

Our country is in terrible chaos now. We wonder if God has damned Russia. Is it possible it will suffer for ever?

The coup had been defeated with little blood, we could have paid much more for the victory. When we discuss the events with our classmates, we ask ourselves: 'Were the sacrifices in vain? Will there be any changes for the better in the life of our country?' We wish to believe in this so much. And we know that a lot depends on us, young people.

Anna, Moscow

WAKING UP TO AN UNKNOWN FUTURE

In ancient times when the sun suddenly disappeared from the sky people called it 'God's punishment' sent down upon them. Ages have passed and again the unity of nature and spirit has shown its power.

On 19 August the sky suddenly became cloudy. A terrible thunderstorm began. Moscow went through two awful, dark foggy days. And then, on the 21st, the sun came out again. Democracy had won. 'Moscow! Russia! Yeltsin!' People shouted in the Lyubanko Square at the meeting to defend the Russian government, freedom and democracy. I had never seen our people behave this way before – they embraced each other in the streets, or kissed each other, or burst into tears, all in the space of a minute. A general euphoria united all Muscovites. Boris Yeltsin grew in stature, his popularity and his strength increasing by the hour, and most other institutions and local authorities immediately accepted his authority. Our country had made the quickest about-turn in its history. No one had expected the coup to end so suddenly. In fact, it ended the way it had begun – unexpectedly and alarmingly.

Nobody knows what it was all about and people are still scared of a repetition, but the coup showed that something had changed in the consciousness of Muscovites. Inspired by the idea of freedom people spontaneously came to the defence of the 'White House'. In the square opposite the building there were more than 1,000 people. And they stayed in the square throughout the night. Armoured cars tried to get to Smolensky Square but were stopped by a crowd of Yeltsin supporters, barricades of lorries that water and clean the streets, buses and trolleybuses, all barring their way. Soldiers dispersed the crowd by firing shots of tracer bullets into the air. The first fatal, tragic accident happened in Kalinin Avenue, near the centre. After shots from the soldiers people set armoured cars on fire. Two of the demonstrators died. People in Moscow were horrified. Progressive democratic television programmes and newspapers were closed. Avenues were crowded with people, talking, arguing, debating.

But if you had watched our television during this time you would only have seen classical ballet. On the main evening news Vremya announcers couldn't look straight at the camera, but glanced shiftily to one side or another as they tried to hide the truth in their eyes that belied the news statements; they did indeed seem to feel very ashamed of the news they had to read. We began to be afraid of saying too much over the telephone and getting letters from abroad. It was like a return to the Stalin years. We were all terrified that we would go back to the years of a military dictatorship.

All over the Soviet Union people worried about the fate of Mikhail Gorbachev and his family in their dacha in the south. First rumours spread that he had been arrested, then that he was seriously ill. But nobody knew the truth. We went through nervous and difficult days. Perhaps the most active part of our population at this time was the students. Different Moscow colleges sent their students to the barricades by the White House. It was a completely spontaneous gesture by these young people; everybody was spurred on to defend the achievements of democracy. A lot of my friends went to the barricades and spent all night there, under the pouring rain.

On the very first day of the coup my friend and I were crossing the bridge that led to the White House. We knew nothing of what had happened; as far as we were concerned it was a normal day. Then, to my astonishment, I saw a huge crowd in front of the White House waving a Russian Democratic Flag. We were not allowed to get any nearer, so we had to turn round, still mystified. And suddenly in front of me I saw a lot of tanks moving towards me – as you can imagine, this is not a pleasant feeling. I noticed that the pavements beside me had been ruined by the caterpillar tracks of tanks. All the time people were just waking up to what was happening. They came out of their houses, transfixed with horror, holding their children tightly. The atmosphere was tense, frightened, but at the same time the people were very angry. There was also the very unpleasant sensation that at any time the guns on the tanks could start firing. My friend and I could not get to the centre of Moscow because the streets were full of people, and there was practically no traffic because of the tanks blocking the roads.

With others, we listened to the radio in a car, with constant broadcasts of news and reports from the new government. All the news was terrible. I turned and went home. And at home I couldn't watch the news, none of us could, and yet we had to, to find out, to try and find out what was happening. When we did watch it we had the feeling that all our hopes had been denied. But then my father went to the barricades. He spent the whole night there, and when he returned we could understand what was really happening. He returned, in fact, on the second day of the coup and said there was nothing to worry about, the coup could not possibly endure because the people around the White House would never let the barricades be taken down until the militarists had left the building.

He was right. Within three days the coup was over. The

sun emerged from the clouds and spread its warmth all over Moscow. The coup had politicised people very quickly and inspired them to a new activism. It had done the reverse of what it had set out to do: it had speeded up the development of democracy and *glasnost* in the USSR.